The Christian Story and its Message

FOR THE MATURING CHRISTIAN

The Naked Apostles
Phil and Colleen Livingston

Published by: The Naked Apostles

WAUCONDA, IL

The Naked Apostles/Phil and Colleen Livingston
304 Barrington Road
Wauconda, IL 60084
www.nakedapostles.org
email: info@nakedapostles.org

Ordering Information:
Quantity sales. Special discounts are available on quantity purchases by corporations, associations, and others. For details, contact the "Special Sales Department" at the address above.

The Christian Story and its Message: *For the Maturing Christian*/The Naked Apostles, Phil and Colleen Livingston. —1st ed..
ISBN 978-0-9960102-1-4

Table of Contents

This book is dedicated to our sons, Isaac, Lucas, Samuel, Noah, Jon, Joseph and Javier. May the message in this story be demonstrated in their lives and spread like fire throughout this generation. Amen.

If you do what is right, will you not be accepted?

— Genesis 4:7 NIV

The Christian Story and its Message

NIV Ge 3:17 To Adam he said, "Because you listened to your wife and ate from the tree about which I commanded you, 'You must not eat of it,' "Cursed is the ground because of you; through painful toil you will eat of it all the days of your life.
NIV Ge 3:18 It will produce thorns and thistles for you, and you will eat the plants of the field.
NIV Ge 3:19 By the sweat of your brow you will eat your food until you return to the ground, since from it you were taken; for dust you are and to dust you will return."

NIV Ge 3:22 And the LORD God said, "The man has now become like one of us, knowing good and evil. He must not be allowed to reach out his hand and take also from the tree of life and eat, and live forever."

Adam sinned and death entered into the world. However, this was not the original plan. Neither Adam nor mankind were meant to die. Our natural bodies were meant to live forever. However, because of Adam, no man born of a woman can escape death.

This raises a lot of questions: Is it true that because he ate (what?) a piece of fruit(?) death entered into the world and has effected every living thing? What was this fruit? What exactly is death? When you die, do you cease to exist, or is it true that a part of man remains alive and only the body dies? If so, what are the different parts of man, and what lives on? Where does it live on if it has no embodiment? The million dollar question throughout history has been, "Why is God holding against us something Adam did?"

These questions turn out to be not only important, but absolutely central to the Christian story. The Christian story is totally centered on what will happen after the premature end of the earth, the natural universe, and every element that makes up matter. This includes all natural embodiments of human beings—flesh made up of the natural elements.

Amp Isa 34:4 *All the host of the heavens shall be dissolved and crumble away, and the skies shall be rolled together like a scroll; and all their host [the stars and the planets] shall drop like a faded leaf from the vine, and like a withered fig from the fig tree.*

Amp 2Pe 3:3 *To begin with, you must know and understand this, that scoffers (mockers) will come in the last days with scoffing, [people who] walk after their own fleshly desires*
Amp 2Pe 3:4 *And say, Where is the promise of His coming? For since the forefathers fell asleep, all things have continued exactly as they did from the beginning of creation.*
Amp 2Pe 3:5 *For they willfully overlook and forget this [fact], that the heavens [came into] existence long ago by the word of God, and the earth also which was formed out of water and by means of water,*
Amp 2Pe 3:6 *Through which the world that then [existed] was deluged with water and perished.*
Amp 2Pe 3:7 *But by the same word the present heavens and earth have been stored up (reserved) for fire, being kept until the day of judgment and destruction of the ungodly people.*
Amp 2Pe 3:8 *Nevertheless, do not let this one fact escape you, beloved, that with the Lord one day is as a thousand years and a thousand years as one day.*
Amp 2Pe 3:9 *The Lord does not delay and is not tardy or slow about what He promises, according to some people's conception of slowness, but He is long-suffering (extraordinarily patient) toward you, not desiring that any should perish, but that all should turn to repentance.*
Amp 2Pe 3:10 *But the day of the Lord will come like a thief, and then the heavens will vanish (pass away) with a thunderous crash, and the [material] elements [of the*

universe] will be dissolved with fire, and the earth and the works that are upon it will be burned up.

Amp 2Pe 3:11 Since all these things are thus in the process of being dissolved, what kind of person ought [each of] you to be [in the meanwhile] in consecrated and holy behavior and devout and godly qualities,

Amp 2Pe 3:12 While you wait and earnestly long for (expect and hasten) the coming of the day of God by reason of which the flaming heavens will be dissolved, and the [material] elements [of the universe] will flare and melt with fire?

Furthermore, and again central to the Christian message is the opportunity for fallen man to avoid an eternal death—a death of disembodiment, a state he lives in for eternity while in torment. The other option is to take advantage of an extended pardon, which will allow the recipient to live in bliss. He will live with his Maker for eternity, clothed in a supernatural embodiment. A body made not of natural matter/elements but that of supernatural matter like those of the angels, impervious to the pain, suffering, hunger, thirst, and yes, even the death sentence given to the natural universe and all of its elements. God is taking for Himself a race of celestial humans from among the natural humans doomed for destruction.

What necessitates becoming a celestial human is that the earth and the natural universe and all of the elements that comprise it are sentenced to burn in the lake of fire. Anything made out of these elements (natural matter) already have a death sentence. So, in order to have an embodiment that will transcend the lake of fire, it must be made up of some other material other than natural matter—the elements of the natural universe.

As we move through time, even upon the end of all things, the contemporary Church as a whole is found to have an astonishing lack of real answers that are pointed, clear, and direct to the questions above. This is pitiful considering that the Church is the keeper of this story and its message. It is their charge to make this story known to all, so that the human race may neither come to the end of their lives nor to the end of time without knowing it. This decided lack includes not only satisfactory answers to those questions above, but the many more we will cover in this book which are also elementary to the message and absolutely essential to understanding it. Questions whose answers explain the basic choices of our individual fates, including all the requirements and circumstances which will allow us to take advantage of our narrow choices.

We will go through this story in a linear way so that it can be understood as a whole story in context to every step God has and is taking to accomplish His plans.

CHAPTER 1

The Fall

A dam and Eve sinned by eating the fruit of the tree of the knowledge of good and evil. In our culture, the fruit is said to be an apple, and thus an apple tree. Men have what is called an Adam's apple in their throat. The reasoning is that Adam choked on his sin. Also the Latin word for "evil" and "apple" are almost identical. In the culture of the Hebrews, the fruit was said to be a fig, and thus a fig tree because Adam and Eve sewed fig leaves together to cover themselves when their eyes were opened and they discovered they were naked. Some have taught that the fruit was a grape and have their reasons wrapped up in the evils of wine. Others, a pomegranate because the origin of the pomegranate is from the Tigris and Euphrates River Valley where the garden of Eden is thought to have been. Others believed mushrooms were the forbidden fruit; they had their reasons just as others reasoned it was wheat. Still yet, others think it was flesh and the fruit was the sex organs and, thus, got Eve pregnant.

As a result, the image in most people's mind is that the tree is a physical fruit tree, and the fruit of the tree of the knowledge of good and evil is a piece of physical fruit. However, in Hebrew, a tree represents a strong leader or a source of nurturing and life. There are many occasions in the Bible in which strong leaders are referred to as trees. In the middle of the garden, it was said, there were two trees. However, there were in fact many physical fruit bearing trees of different kinds. Adam and Eve were said to have eaten or ingested the fruit of the tree of the knowledge of good and evil. It did not say that they ate the fruit of the apple tree.

Jesus, the tree of life (the other tree), said He is the bread of life and that we must drink His blood and eat His flesh to have eternal life. We must ingest His words into our hearts, words which He said of are Spirit, and we must get our power to live from them. As such, we learn that one of the two trees is a being and not a plant (Jesus/the Word of God). Why would it not be the same for the other of the two trees? The Bible tells us it is the same for the evil tree as it is for ingesting the bread of life. In that when Eve decided to ingest it, she saw that it was desirable for gaining wisdom.

NIV Ge 3:6 *When the woman saw that the fruit of the tree was good for food and pleasing to the eye, and also desirable for gaining wisdom, she took some and ate it.*

To desire to eat something in a spiritual sense is to desire knowledge of it. To chew and ingest it is to understand it and how to use it. Food in the natural realm is fruit or something we chew and ingest into the body to gain power to act. Food in the spirit realm is knowledge we chew on or understand its usefulness, and then accept/approve in our hearts and use its power to act on. Fruit from a fruit tree is food and life for the body; wisdom from a celestial leader (a tree) is food and life for the spirit and soul (mind). Both are required to sustain the whole of man's three natures as Jesus tells us (below).

NIV Mt 4:4 *Jesus answered, "It is written: 'Man does not live on bread alone, but on every word that comes from the mouth of God.'"*

At the end, when Satan—the Devil—is thrown into the lake of fire for eternity, there is only one tree left in the New Jerusalem, and that is the tree of life—Jesus.

NLT Eze 28:12 *... You were the perfection of wisdom and beauty.*
NLT Eze 28:13 *You were in Eden, the garden of God. Your clothing was adorned with every precious stone —red carnelian, chrysolite, white moonstone, beryl, onyx, jasper, sapphire, turquoise, and emerald—all beautifully crafted for you and set in the finest gold. They were given to you on the day you were created.*
NLT Eze 28:14 *I ordained and anointed you as the mighty angelic guardian. You had access to the holy mountain of God and walked among the stones of fire.*
NLT Eze 28:15 *"You were blameless in all you did from the day you were created until the day evil was found in you.*
NLT Eze 28:16 *Your great wealth filled you with violence, and you sinned. So I banished you from the mountain of God. I expelled you, O mighty guardian, from your place among the stones of fire.*
NLT Eze 28:17 *Your heart was filled with pride because of all your beauty. You corrupted your wisdom for the sake of your splendor. So I threw you to the earth ...*

We see that God had placed Satan in the garden of Eden. It goes on to say he was anointed a guardian of Eden and furthermore had access also to the throne of God in Heaven, even among the fiery stones before God's throne. However, at one point He was found to have become corrupt. It was clear he did not start out that way. Once he did become corrupt, he lost his place in heaven before God and was expelled, losing access to the throne. Although Satan still had a place in the garden, it is reasonable to believe that he lost his authority as the mighty angelic guardian.

How can this be said? The Bible says he lost his place and status in heaven where his authority was issued. It also is revealed, after Adam's creation when God talked to him about the middle of the garden, that there were two trees. Perhaps once the one became corrupt and no longer had access to the throne of God, a second angelic or celestial guardian was needed who did have access to the throne of God, and there became two as a result. One having the authority to give life, the other divided from God offering only death. The garden may have remained his habitat after losing his place in heaven, but he was stripped of his former authority and position in it.

In addition to that, when God created Adam, God gave him charge of the garden to work it, and he was given dominion (authority) over it. Is it not reasonable to assume that this was a portion of the former authority Satan was stripped of? Then he was told he could eat fruit from the one tree of life which (obviously) had access to the throne, because it would give him life. Adam was furthermore admonished not to ingest the fruit of the knowledge of good and evil from the other tree, because it would bring death. This was a result of no longer having access to the throne, while in rebellion to God.

NIV Ge 2:7 the LORD God formed the man from the dust of the ground and breathed into his nostrils the breath of life, and the man became a living being.
NIV Ge 2:8 Now the LORD God had planted a garden in the east, in Eden; and there he put the man he had formed.
NIV Ge 2:9 And the LORD God made all kinds of trees grow out of the ground—trees that were pleasing to the eye and good for food. In the middle of the garden were the tree of life and the tree of the knowledge of good and evil.

NIV Ge 2:15 *The LORD God took the man and put him in the Garden of Eden to work it and take care of it.*

NIV Ge 2:16 *And the LORD God commanded the man, "You are free to eat from any tree in the garden;*

NIV Ge 2:17 *but you must not eat from the tree of the knowledge of good and evil, for when you eat of it you will surely die."*

The Bible tells us that Satan was in the garden before Adam, and he became corrupt before Adam was created. Perhaps the jealousy Satan had was because he was stripped of his authority in the garden, and that authority was given to a man, Adam. This fueled his rivalry and hatred of humankind.

What this means is that it was not an apple, but the rebellious knowledge or awareness that one could live independent from God and outside His authority simply by not obeying Him. How do we know that the evil knowledge was to understand you could live independent from God and outside His authority? Because it was a corrupt, wisdom-based knowledge of evil (disobedience). That being the case, the persuasion used to induce them into ingesting this knowledge of good and evil was that God was holding something back from them, and if they possessed this forbidden or secret knowledge they could be like God. In other words, they could be independent and free to be gods themselves, being the center of all things.

NIV Ge 3:1 *Now the serpent was more crafty than any of the wild animals the LORD God had made. He said to the woman, "Did God really say, 'You must not eat from any tree in the garden'?"*

NIV Ge 3:2 *The woman said to the serpent, "We may eat fruit from the trees in the garden,*

NIV Ge 3:3 *but God did say, 'You must not eat fruit from the tree that is in the middle of the garden, and you must not touch it, or you will die.'"*

NIV Ge 3:4 *"You will not surely die," the serpent said to the woman.*

NIV Ge 3:5 *"For God knows that when you eat of it your eyes will be opened, and you will be like God, knowing good and evil."*

NIV Ge 3:6 *When the woman saw that the fruit of the tree was good for food and pleasing to the eye, and also desirable for gaining wisdom, she took some and ate it. She also gave some to her husband, who was with her, and he ate it.*

It is common knowledge that the Devil, also known as Satan, was behind the fall of man. However, in the Biblical narrative, all we really hear about is the serpent seducing Eve into ingesting the knowledge of good and evil from the fruit of this tree. One has to ask, "If this is from the Devil, where then is the Devil in the story?" The answer is, the serpent may have seduced Eve into partaking of the tree, but the tree was the Devil.

How does what they did affect me and why does God hold it against me?

We understand that original sin is the cause of our downfall, but it is not that common to study its effect on mankind. Adam and Eve sinned by ingesting the fruit of the knowledge of good and evil. The deciding factor that made ingesting this knowledge appealing was that they could be gods unto themselves—just like God Almighty. Although ingesting the fruit of the knowledge of good and evil gave us an outlook on life as if we were God, we still lack the power God has, to be God. If anyone were asked if they thought they were God, they would say, "No, of course not!" However, according to our human spirit perception (wisdom), which we received from Adam, we see everything from the standpoint as if we were God.

NIV Gen 3:5 *. . . when you eat of it your eyes will be opened, and you will be like God, knowing good and evil . . .*

What does this have to do with wisdom? Well, wisdom is like the software on a computer. Without it, all the information stored in its memory may as well not be there. The software is needed to understand what it sees (the memory on the hard drive) as being something. It's the same with the spirit of man, which is awareness. It needs software to understand what it sees as being something.

That needed software the Bible calls, "wisdom." Wisdom can be defined as a set of values by which to perceive through. Wisdom and its resulting perception is a faculty of the spirit. That being the case, wisdom functions from a place beyond words—in our very essence. It is only after we have a spirit perception (outlook) and feelings about a thing that words, reasoning, and rationalization of the soul can begin to work, giving us thoughts and emotions with words about that thing. Spirit does not think and understand with words as our mind does.

God endowed the spirit of each kind of creature with a unique wisdom. The wisdom God endowed in man was much different than the wisdom He gave animals and angels, for example.

Wisdom can also be acquired through life experiences. The soul can change (its mind) with words or concepts. But this is beyond the spirit's ability to do so. Spirit is memory. The spirit changes experientially, since it understands things through its experiences. That being the case, through experience one's wisdom can increase.

The secondary reason Adam and Eve consumed or ingested the fruit of the knowledge of good and evil is revealed in this verse:

NIV Ge 3:6 When the woman saw that the fruit of the tree was good for food and pleasing to the eye, and also desirable for gaining wisdom, she took some and ate it. She also gave some to her husband, who was with her, and he ate it.

It is important to take note here that wisdom has come up in the Bible, in three key places. In the verse above it states, the Devil "corrupted his wisdom." Now that Adam and Eve have joined him in the garden, it says she thought the fruit was desirable for "gaining wisdom." We see by the account of the fall that wisdom was gained by eating the fruit of the knowledge of good and evil. In other words, a set of values by which to perceive through was ingested that would make one aware of the fact that there was an alternative to obeying God, which is nonconformity to God (evil).

As simple as that concept might seem to us, ignorance of that awareness/perception was certainly bliss. Eve thought it would give her the required wisdom (spiritual outlook—perception) needed to be like God. In reality, she was ingesting the spirit of the Devil, which was corrupt and wanted to be god, independent of the real God.

Amp Eze 28:17 Your heart was proud and lifted up because of your beauty; you corrupted your wisdom for the sake of your splendor.

Again, the word wisdom appears both in what was corrupt about the spirit of the Devil, and what Eve wanted to gain in ingesting that wisdom of the Devil. The fruit of the knowledge of good and evil, with its wisdom values, is a wisdom of the Devil, which he had corrupted to rebel against God and raise himself above Him. In James talking about the two trees in the garden, which he refers to as the two different wisdoms, he say of the one wisdom (or tree):

NIV Jas 3:15 Such "wisdom" does not come down from heaven but is earthly, unspiritual, of the devil.

The wisdom from the tree that bares the fruit of the knowledge of good and evil which is the Devil and the former guardian of the garden, James proclaims that wisdom is "of the Devil". It is the wisdom or logic of the

Devil that Eve desired to ingest, thinking somehow it would profit her to possess.

Here is a third time that wisdom is mentioned in this context: Jesus called Himself the bread of life, and the true manna that comes down from heaven. These sayings of Jesus are explained more clearly by James, when he spoke about the opposing tree or as he says, the "wisdom that comes down from heaven (Jas 3:17)." Now we can understand why Jesus said you must eat my body and drink my blood, my body is real food and my blood real drink. To do so is to reverse the effect of eating the fruit of the knowledge of good and evil.

1. The Devil corrupted his wisdom.
2. Eve desired his corrupt wisdom thinking it would gain her something special, then ingested it.
3. Jesus brings down from heaven a wisdom for us to ingest which is a correcting wisdom.

In saying whoever eats His body and drinks His blood will never die, Jesus is talking in line with how the story in Genesis was written. They ate of the fruit from the tree of the knowledge of good and evil, and, in doing so, brought death because of its disconnected rebellious status with the source of life. Conversely, to ingest Jesus brings life eternal. Again, Jesus is presenting a solution to the original problem/sin, which affirms it was not an apple they ate. In another reference to these two trees in the garden, Jesus taught His disciples that you cannot get good fruit from a bad tree and you cannot get bad fruit from a good tree.

Adam and Eve took on the spirit wisdom of the Devil (the "bad" tree) with his corrupt wisdom values, and it corrupted their spirit perception, causing them to see themselves as if they were God. Therefore, they forever corrupted the human spirit, which we receive from the father of the human race, Adam. To ingest the Spirit of Jesus (the "good" tree) and

His wisdom is to correct what is wrong from ingesting (into the human spirit) the Devil's. By calling Himself the bread of life, Jesus was literally talking in answer to what happened in the garden as it was recorded in the Bible.

Below is the effect our corrupt wisdom values have on our spirit perception so that we unconsciously perceive ourselves as if we are God.

We are:

1) Self-conscious
2) Self-centered
3) Self-sustaining
4) Self-determined
5) Self-serving
6) Self-gratifying

In general, we have a world view that sees everything as originating and ending with self.

When we see the world from a perspective of the above list, it gives us an erroneous outlook and skews our understanding, no matter how intelligent we are. As James says, we are, "In defiance of and false to the truth (Amp Jas 3:14)." Let us look at these one at a time.

1. We are self-conscious instead of being God-conscious.

We see, feel, and experience everything in light of how it affects us, in a hyper-sensitive way. We no longer see and experience others and circumstances as they truly are—something that is centered around God and not us.

We see the first evidence of this recorded in the Bible when Adam and Eve hid from God, self-conscious that they were naked.

NIV Ge 3:9-11 *But the LORD God called to the man, "Where are you?" He answered, "I heard you in the garden, and I was afraid because I was naked; so I hid." And he said, "Who told you that you were naked? Have you eaten from the tree that I commanded you not to eat from?"*

2. We are self-centered instead of being God-centered.

We no longer see the universe as revolving around God and His purposes, but as revolving around us individually and our own purposes, desires, and emotions.

3. Self-sustaining

We see our lives as something we alone sustain and preserve. If we don't sustain our lives, we believe we will perish. We no longer see God as the one who sustains, provides, and preserves our lives, (but we believe we have to look out for number one).

The Christian reading this might say, "But I rely on God." Just as we stated above, if asked, "Do you think you are God?" People would answer, "Heavens no!" We then point out that even though someone would respond this way with their intelligence, because of the corruptness of the human spirit, the very same person has a world view perceiving everything (in that place beyond words) as if he was God. His spirit outlook is in conflict with his understanding.

Likewise, it is the same for the Christian that says from an intellectual standpoint, "I rely on God." He might decide to understand things that way, but without a change of spirit, his corrupt spirit has a world view in that place beyond words perceiving things as if it was him alone who sustains his life. Thus, he is constantly tempted into taking matters into his own hands and finally justifying them to God, instead of waiting upon God and His wisdom.

4. Self-determined

We become self-willed: inventing our own purposes for our lives, blind to God's divine will and purpose for our lives. We become the judge and determine all things. We decide what is right and what is wrong. The only problem here is not only do we see everything with a "me, myself, and I" filter on our perception, but we also have very little information and insight into any situation as to how it fits into the bigger picture. Nor is our perception in line with the purposes God had in mind when creating each individual.

5. Self-serving

Our interest is to first preserve our own lives, purposes, and desires as we understand them. We see and process everything in this light. We see everything in light of how everything and everyone is either a threat to us or serves us, enhances our world or takes away from it, helps us or hurts us. We no longer see things or people for what they truly are, but what they are in light of our own lives, purposes, and desires. Although this may seem merely self-preserving, it has a huge debilitating affect on our perception of others and the reality of all circumstances.

6. Self-gratifying

We look to and are mainly concerned with gratifying ourselves instead of gratifying God. We are lovers of ourselves and live to serve our own desires. We do not spend our lives primarily on the objects of our love (the way of heaven) but on ourselves. You could say we are our first love.

7. A world view that sees everything as originating from self.

Everything we sense we primarily and mistakenly perceive as coming out of us. This includes feelings, thoughts, desires, and motives, whether or not they are being generated by God, celestial beings, or other people. We see everything as beginning with us and our participation in a matter, and ending with us and our role in that matter. However, life goes on without us.

It is important to understand that before Adam and Eve ate the fruit of the tree of the knowledge of good and evil, they could do anything their imagination could come up with and never sin or offend God. The tree in the middle of the garden was not like a loaded gun in a room full of children and telling them not to touch it, then leaving the room. For children of corrupt man, that would be stirring up their curiosity, causing them to wonder why they should not touch the gun, or what was it about the gun that made it wrong to have. It would actually cause them to wonder and pick it up, wanting to know.

However, for Adam and Eve, when God commanded them not to eat of the fruit of the tree in the middle of the garden, they simply did not eat. They were naive. They had no subjective reasoning to tell them that there was an actual option besides obeying God which we now know is to not obey Him. This would never occur to them. He commanded not to and they simply did not and had nothing in them to cause them to consider they should. They had only knowledge of good. Knowledge of evil was not in their wisdom paradigm, and thus they were naive to even consider it.

It seems strange to us that they didn't have a covetousness inside of them and a desire to have something that God did not give them. Furthermore, it seems very strange indeed that it was beyond the realm of their wisdom/perception to have an inability to be curious or a desire to know why they shouldn't.

The fact that it is almost inconceivable and odd to us that it wasn't within them to question God, or to be curious why not, or to want something outside of what God gave them, verifies about us that our nature is corrupt. It is natural for us to want to explore the gun simply because we are told not to.

Before the fall, if God left loaded guns in a room and then departed, commanding them not to touch them, it would be as if the guns weren't even there; they would have no interest in them, and nothing would draw their attention towards them. It would be perfectly safe for God to leave the room after having commanded them to not touch them. This is because, again, it was inconceivable for them; there was no alternative but to do what God commanded.

Someone or something had to introduce this concept to them for them to even know it. Someone who had discovered how to live independent of God as well as adopt a wisdom with a perception which gave them a knowledge that there was an alternative to obeying God. That's why it is said that it is the "fruit of the knowledge of good and evil." This knowledge/wisdom gave them subjective reasoning, causing them to doubt and question God and be curious about why they should obey God.

It is an awesome responsibility to have this knowledge, for it causes men to constantly disobey God and search out life independent from Him. Desiring to know what it means to be outside of what God gives them is "the grass is greener on the other side of the hill" syndrome. Indeed, life would be much easier if this piece of wisdom (knowledge of evil) was never ingested into the spirit of Adam. There would be no temptation or any subjective reasoning saying that there was an alternative outside of what God has given to us. Neither would we invent our own destinies. Thus, we would be content with what we have and naive to anything outside of that. Nor would we be driven by spirit motives to have what is outside of what God has given to us. Yes, the Devil did us a disservice.

Two other things happened at that tree, on that day, that are important to mention. The way the serpent seduced Eve and Adam was to make them believe, first, that God couldn't be trusted, and, second, He was holding back something from them that they should have or desire to have. He imparted to them a spirit of covetousness (a jealousy for what you do not have) and an entitlement to have what others have without working for or paying the price for it.

NIV Ge 3:3-5 but God did say, 'You must not eat fruit from the tree that is in the middle of the garden, and you must not touch it, or you will die.' " "You will not surely die," the serpent said to the woman. "For God knows that when you eat of it your eyes will be opened, and you will be like God, knowing good and evil."

The part of our being that hears God's Spirit (primarily without words) and receives His instructions is our conscience. Our conscience is a faculty of our soul that helps us discern spirit feelings as good or bad, right or wrong. When it is working, uncorrupted by the fall, it is followed and trusted above our intellect (which is also a faculty of our soul). A very significant change happened when Adam took on the corrupt spirit of the Devil. It was a spirit that changed all the rules in a huge way, and those changes in perception now seem normal.

We went from:

Using our intellect to understand what we sense from God, translating the spirit feelings into words for our mind to grasp, and using the intellect to *see how* what we are sensing from Him is true and right.

To:

Using our intellect *to judge* whether or not what we are sensing from God is true or right.

From the time of the fall since Adam believed from the serpent that God wasn't trustworthy, we believe we can only trust our intellect. We may say we trust God, but, in the end, it is our own intellect we really trust. We believe that it knows better what is right or wrong, since it thinks in terms of self, and of itself as God. This is a result of a corrupt spirit perception of self.

As a result of this corrupt spirit perception, as we grow up and mature, we learn to judge and discern with our intellect. In doing so we grow in invalidating, overruling, and dismissing what God is telling us through our conscience (which again is from a place beyond words). We trust our intellect to decide what is right and what is good through reasoning and rationalizing with word knowledge. Our hearts are thus hardened to God and our conscience becomes ignored in preference of figuring things out with our mind.

A most common saying that supports this and makes it normal to process this way is: "God gave you a brain, now use it." However, the Bible tells us that Jesus is for us, our wisdom from God.

NIV 1Co 1:30 It is because of him that you are in Christ Jesus, who has become for us wisdom from God—that is, our righteousness, holiness and redemption.

NIV 1Co 1:31 Therefore, as it is written: "Let him who boasts boast in the Lord."

NIV 1Co 2:1 When I came to you, brothers, I did not come with eloquence or superior wisdom as I proclaimed to you the testimony about God.

NIV 1Co 2:2 For I resolved to know nothing while I was with you except Jesus Christ and him crucified.

NIV 1Co 2:3 I came to you in weakness and fear, and with much trembling.

NIV 1Co 2:4 My message and my preaching were not with wise and persuasive words, but with a demonstration of the Spirit's power,

NIV 1Co 2:5 so that your faith might not rest on men's wisdom, but on God's power.

Wisdom From the Spirit

NIV 1Co 2:6 We do, however, speak a message of wisdom among the mature, but not the wisdom of this age or of the rulers of this age, who are coming to nothing.

NIV 1Co 2:7 No, we speak of God's secret wisdom, a wisdom that has been hidden and that God destined for our glory before time began.

NIV 1Co 2:8 *None of the rulers of this age understood it, for if they had, they would not have crucified the Lord of glory.*

NIV 1Co 2:9 *However, as it is written: "No eye has seen, no ear has heard, no mind has conceived what God has prepared for those who love him"* . . .

NIV 1Co 2:10 *but God has revealed it to us by his Spirit.*

This is one of the hardest stumbling blocks we run into when trying to teach someone to be a spiritual man: to follow their conscience that comes in the form of spirit feelings, instincts, and perceptions. They must do this instead of reasoning and rationalizing with words what they think is right or wrong. People just don't trust not using their intellect to sort things out. Even if they are intuitive and hear God, they still have to have a reason and see it as something good before they can believe or trust their conscience. They think it is foolish and irresponsible to be led by the Spirit as opposed to the intellect. However, what they are unwittingly doing is not trusting God's Spirit within them, but instead their own intellect.

Amp 1Co 2:6 *Yet when we are among the full-grown (spiritually mature Christians who are ripe in understanding), we do impart a [higher] wisdom (the knowledge of the divine plan previously hidden); but it is indeed not a wisdom of this present age or of this world nor of the leaders and rulers of this age, who are being brought to nothing and are doomed to pass away.*

Amp 1Co 2:14 *But the natural, nonspiritual man does not accept or welcome or admit into his heart the gifts and teachings and revelations of the Spirit of God, for they are folly (meaningless nonsense) to him; and he is incapable of knowing them because they are spiritually discerned and estimated and appreciated.*

Getting back to the fall of man

Death has entered into the natural world because of Adam. It is a spiritual death, a separation from God, much the same as it was for the Devil. However, this spiritual death also has an effect on the human body, unlike it does to the celestial body of the Devil. It brings a death of decay until the body ceases to live. It does not kill the flesh right away but causes it to degenerate and decay until it dies and the soul can be clothed with it no more. The spirit and souls of humanity cannot cease to exist, but can die a death which means separation from God for eternity.

However, to the body (the flesh man is clothed with) it dies a death which causes it to cease to exist, and it returns back to the elements from which it came. This leaves the soul of the man—which is the real man, his personality—naked (unclothed, disembodied) forever and separated from God. For humans, this is what death means.

This became the fate of all flesh, the children of Adam, because of his sin. This was a terrible consequence of ingesting into the first man's spirit the rebellious spirit wisdom of the Devil and his knowledge of good and evil. Nevertheless, the human spirit, passed on to all of Adam's offspring, was forever corrupted by it being opened up to that wisdom. The outlook of man was forever changed, and, indeed, his eyes were opened and death entered in.

Through no fault of God's or of their own, the children of Adam are born with a corrupt spirit wisdom (outlook). As a result, the corrupt outlook of the human spirit causes all to sin and rebel against God. All suffer the same eternal fate of separation from God and becoming a soul no longer clothed in a body, but disembodied forever. It is a terrible state for the invisible nature of man to have no expression, outlet, or manifestation through an embodiment.

However, God, in his mercy even before the first man died, made a way for Adam and his children, humankind. For the souls who die to their body but live on as a soul (mind), he created a temporary place to hold and confine them, until the last day of the earth. That place is called the Hades, or Sheol (Hebrew). On the last day, all humans ever born will have lost their bodies.

On the last day and because of the corruptness brought about by man, God will destroy the natural universe and all its elements along with all matter, throwing it into what is called, "The lake of fire." This is the current and unchangeable fate of the natural universe. By the judgment of God, not only man, but the world he lives in will be destroyed. Man lives ignorantly under a death sentence because his spirit has been corrupted. It is a verdict already sealed.

This event will leave all the remaining souls of men, who are alive on the earth at that time, naked and unclothed—a soul without a body. The reason is: the body is comprised of natural elements, which will perish.

Amp 2Pe 3:3 To begin with, you must know and understand this, that scoffers (mockers) will come in the last days with scoffing, [people who] walk after their own fleshly desires

Amp 2Pe 3:4 And say, Where is the promise of His coming? For since the forefathers fell asleep, all things have continued exactly as they did from the beginning of creation.

Amp 2Pe 3:5 For they willfully overlook and forget this [fact], that the heavens [came into] existence long ago by the word of God, and the earth also which was formed out of water and by means of water,

Amp 2Pe 3:6 Through which the world that then [existed] was deluged with water and perished.

Amp 2Pe 3:7 But by the same word the present heavens and earth have been stored up (reserved) for fire, being kept until the day of judgment and destruction of the ungodly people.

Amp 2Pe 3:8 *Nevertheless, do not let this one fact escape you, beloved, that with the Lord one day is as a thousand years and a thousand years as one day.*

Amp 2Pe 3:9 *The Lord does not delay and is not tardy or slow about what He promises, according to some people's conception of slowness, but He is long-suffering (extraordinarily patient) toward you, not desiring that any should perish, but that all should turn to repentance.*

Amp 2Pe 3:10 *But the day of the Lord will come like a thief, and then the heavens will vanish (pass away) with a thunderous crash, and the [material] elements [of the universe] will be dissolved with fire, and the earth and the works that are upon it will be burned up.*

Amp 2Pe 3:11 *Since all these things are thus in the process of being dissolved, what kind of person ought [each of] you to be [in the meanwhile] in consecrated and holy behavior and devout and godly qualities,*

Amp 2Pe 3:12 *While you wait and earnestly long for (expect and hasten) the coming of the day of God by reason of which the flaming heavens will be dissolved, and the [material] elements [of the universe] will flare and melt with fire?*

Amp 2Pe 3:13 *But we look for new heavens and a new earth according to His promise, in which righteousness (uprightness, freedom from sin, and right standing with God) is to abide.*

Amp 2Pe 3:14 *So, beloved, since you are expecting these things, be eager to be found by Him [at His coming] without spot or blemish and at peace [in serene confidence, free from fears and agitating passions and moral conflicts].*

Amp 2Pe 3:15 *And consider that the long-suffering of our Lord [His slowness in avenging wrongs and judging the world] is salvation (that which is conducive to the soul's safety) . . .*

Jesus too speaks of this day:

NIV Jn 5:26 *For as the Father has life in himself, so he has granted the Son to have life in himself.*

NIV Jn 5:27 *And he has given him authority to judge because he is the Son of Man.*

NIV Jn 5:28 *"Do not be amazed at this, for a time is coming when all who are in their graves will hear his voice*

NIV Jn 5:29 *and come out—those who have done good will rise to live, and those who have done evil will rise to be condemned.*

NIV Jn 5:30 *By myself I can do nothing; I judge only as I hear, and my judgment is just, for I seek not to please myself but him who sent me.*

NIV Mt 25:31 *"When the Son of Man comes in his glory, and all the angels with him, he will sit on his throne in heavenly glory.*

NIV Mt 25:32 *All the nations will be gathered before him, and he will separate the people one from another as a shepherd separates the sheep from the goats.*

NIV Mt 25:33 *He will put the sheep on his right and the goats on his left.*

NIV Mt 25:34 *"Then the King will say to those on his right, 'Come, you who are blessed by my Father; take your inheritance, the kingdom prepared for you since the creation of the world.*

NIV Mt 25:35 *For I was hungry and you gave me something to eat, I was thirsty and you gave me something to drink, I was a stranger and you invited me in,*

NIV Mt 25:36 *I needed clothes and you clothed me, I was sick and you looked after me, I was in prison and you came to visit me.'*

NIV Mt 25:37 *"Then the righteous will answer him, 'Lord, when did we see you hungry and feed you, or thirsty and give you something to drink?*

NIV Mt 25:38 *When did we see you a stranger and invite you in, or needing clothes and clothe you?*

NIV Mt 25:39 *When did we see you sick or in prison and go to visit you?'*

NIV Mt 25:40 *"The King will reply, 'I tell you the truth, whatever you did for one of the least of these brothers of mine, you did for me.'*

NIV Mt 25:41 *"Then he will say to those on his left, 'Depart from me, you who are cursed, into the eternal fire prepared for the devil and his angels.*

NIV Mt 25:42 *For I was hungry and you gave me nothing to eat, I was thirsty and you gave me nothing to drink,*

NIV Mt 25:43 *I was a stranger and you did not invite me in, I needed clothes and you did not clothe me, I was sick and in prison and you did not look after me.'*

NIV Mt 25:44 *"They also will answer, 'Lord, when did we see you hungry or thirsty or a stranger or needing clothes or sick or in prison, and did not help you?'*

NIV Mt 25:45 "*He will reply, 'I tell you the truth, whatever you did not do for one of the least of these, you did not do for me.'*
NIV Mt 25:46 "*Then they will go away to eternal punishment, but the righteous to eternal life.*

However, the mercy of God and the hope of the individual man is this: once everyone ever born has died to his body and exists as a soul unclothed, God will raise them all from the dead (from their disembodied state) and call them out of Hades, giving them a body so they can stand before Him to be judged. Then, He will give them all the same chance before condemning them to a second death. Meaning, all will be judged while facing the prospects of having to once again become unclothed, a disembodied soul. In other words, to be thrown alive into the lake of fire, suffering a second death.

It is then, at that judgment, that the individual soul can escape the fate the first man, Adam, brought upon all men: eternal disembodiment and confinement in the lake of fire, separated from his Maker. Clothed once again with a body, the individual will face his Maker and be judged; this time not by what Adam did, but by the deeds he did—how he conducted himself during his time in the world.

The first death is because of Adam, the second death is solely on the shoulders of the individual and how he conducted himself in life. If your deeds are acceptable to God, you will live on forever in a new incorruptible celestial body, becoming a celestial human, never to die again. If your deeds while clothed in the body find you wanting before God your judge, a second but eternal death will you endure. Then, when it is said and done, there will be no need for the Hades, for it has been emptied, and it too, will be thrown into the lake of fire.

It should be noted about Hades that there is more than one destination within it. Those whose deeds will be judged as acceptable on the last day and who will go on to eternal life, will be unclothed souls (disembodied) confined to a place called paradise—or Abraham's bosom, as Jesus calls it. He spoke of it to the thief on the cross next to Him while they were being crucified. Jesus told the man that today he will be in paradise with Him.

NAS LK 16:22 "*Now the poor man died and was carried away by the angels to Abraham's bosom...*

Amp Lk 23:42 *Then he said to Jesus, Lord, remember me when You come in Your kingly glory!*
Amp Lk 23:43 *And He answered him, Truly I tell you, today you shall be with Me in Paradise.*

Some may say that when Jesus said "in paradise," He meant in heaven with Him and His Father. However, this cannot be true, because three days after He died, He instructed Mary not to hold Him, because He had not yet gone to His Father in heaven.

Amp Jn 20:17 *Jesus said to her, Do not cling to Me [do not hold Me], for I have not yet ascended to the Father.*

He had told the man on the cross next to him, "Today you shall be with Me in Paradise." Paradise/Abraham's bosom is the confinement within Hades that is for the disembodied souls who will be judged acceptable on the last day. It is there Jesus brought the man who was next to Him, and not to heaven before His Father. This same place in Hades is also called, "under the altar of God."

When it was said in the Bible that Jesus would die, go to the place of the dead (hell, Hades, the realm of the dead), break open the gates and lead the captives or prisoners free, this is where He went.

NIV 1Pe 3:18 For Christ died for sins once for all, the righteous for the unrighteous, to bring you to God. He was put to death in the body but made alive by the Spirit, *NIV 1Pe 3:19* through whom also he went and preached to the spirits in prison

NIV 1Pe 3:21 ... by the resurrection of Jesus Christ, *NIV 1Pe 3:22* who has gone into heaven and is at God's right hand —with angels, authorities and powers in submission to him.

The prisoners Jesus set free from the paradisiacal place in Hades were the 144,000 who were under the altar of God and were given white robes.

NIV Rev 6:9 When he opened the fifth seal, I saw under the altar the souls of those who had been slain because of the word of God and the testimony they had maintained. *NIV Rev 6:10* They called out in a loud voice, "How long, Sovereign Lord, holy and true, until you judge the inhabitants of the earth and avenge our blood?" *NIV Rev 6:11* Then each of them was given a white robe ...

The fifth seal was the event of Jesus doing His redeeming work on the cross.

NIV Rev 14:1 Then I looked, and there before me was the Lamb, standing on Mount Zion, and with him 144,000 who had his name and his Father's name written on their foreheads.

Both groups, the souls under the altar of God and the 144,000, are one and the same. Both are spoken of as the first fruits. In verses 6:9-11, those who were under the altar of God were the first to be clothed with a celestial body (given a white robe) and therefore, are able to stand before the throne of God. The 144,000 are called the first fruits of many who would be redeemed. This indicates that they were the first to be clothed with celestial bodies as a result of the redeeming work of the cross. Jesus is called the Lamb standing on Mount Zion in verse 14:1 because He had been sacrificed and now His redeeming work bears its first fruits—the 144,000 who waited to be set free and are now with Him where He is.

NIV Rev 14:2 *And I heard a sound from heaven like the roar of rushing waters and like a loud peal of thunder. The sound I heard was like that of harpists playing their harps.*

NIV Rev 14:3 *And they sang a new song before the throne and before the four living creatures and the elders. No one could learn the song except the 144,000 who had been redeemed from the earth.*

NIV Rev 14:4 *These are those who did not defile themselves with women, for they kept themselves pure. They follow the Lamb wherever he goes. They were purchased from among men and offered as firstfruits to God and the Lamb.*

NIV Rev 14:5 *No lie was found in their mouths; they are blameless.*

The white robes these disembodied souls were given to be clothed with are their celestial bodies, which allow them to stand before God as celestial humans. Jesus set them free from being unclothed souls in prison. These were the first fruits of His redeeming death on the cross. It says of these first fruits that came out of Hades:

NIV Mt 27:50 *And when Jesus had cried out again in a loud voice, he gave up his spirit.*

NIV Mt 27:51 *At that moment the curtain of the temple was torn in two from top to bottom. The earth shook and the rocks split.*

NIV Mt 27:52 *The tombs broke open and the bodies of many holy people who had died were raised to life.*

NIV Mt 27:53 *They came out of the tombs, and after Jesus' resurrection they went into the holy city and appeared to many people.*

The next compartment in Hades is for those who will be judged on the last day and found wanting. They will then be condemned to a second death. This compartment in Hades is called hell, or Gehenna.

Note: there are occasions when the lake of fire is also referred to as hell or Gehenna. But for the sake of this study these terms are not the eternal lake of fire but the place of suffering in Hades.

When David conquered Jerusalem and made it the holy city, there was a place just outside of the city in a valley where the conquered people would worship. At that place, there was an altar where the Canaanites sacrificed children to their god, Moloch. This made the ground of this place so defiled, that the Jews would not build on it or use it.

This place was called Gehenna, the Valley of Hinnom's Son. So instead, they used it as a place to throw the dead bodies of criminals who were executed, as well as those who were denied a proper burial. It was also the city's garbage dump, which was the only use they could justify for the ground. They would burn the refuse to make room for more and to keep down the stench. As a result, the fire never went out or was extinguished. It seemed to be fueled indefinitely. Considering this, Gehenna was adopted as an allegory for the fires of hell and the place for the sinful dead. Jesus Himself used it to give people a visual picture of hell.

They are held, disembodied, in a place of torment, awaiting the last day of judgment when they will be raised from the dead, judged and thrown alive into the lake of fire to endure a second but permanent death.

NAS LK 16:22 *. . . and the rich man also died and was buried.*
NAS LK 16:23 *"In Hades he lifted up his eyes, being in torment, and saw Abraham far away and Lazarus in his bosom.*
NAS LK 16:24 *"And he cried out and said, 'Father Abraham, have mercy on me, and send Lazarus so that he may dip the tip of his finger in water and cool off my tongue, for I am in agony in this flame.'*

NAS LK 16:25 *"But Abraham said, 'Child, remember that during your life you received your good things, and likewise Lazarus bad things; but now he is being comforted here, and you are in agony.*

NAS LK 16:26 *'And besides all this, between us and you there is a great chasm fixed, so that those who wish to come over from here to you will not be able, and that none may cross over from there to us.'*

There is a third place spoken of in Hades; it is for the worst of the worst. It is called the Abyss, or the bottomless pit. We are told that in the future the beast will come up out of the Abyss and live again on his way to his destruction. It also says that after the battle of Armageddon the Devil will be locked away in it for 1,000 years.

Amp 2Pe 2:4 *For God did not [even] spare angels that sinned, but cast them into hell, delivering them to be kept there in pits of gloom till the judgment and their doom.*

Amp 2Pe 2:9 *Now if [all these things are true, then be sure] the Lord knows how to rescue the godly out of temptations and trials, and how to keep the ungodly under chastisement until the day of judgment and doom...*

This is the plan and fairness of God to all who, through no fault of their own, have death as their fate because of the fall. God has provided a way that is fair to all! This is the bases of all that has happened to mankind, and all that has been decided, which will bring to an end the human story by the judgment of God. This is an unchangeable fate for humankind. Everything else is built on or around this justice and judgment of God. The rest of the Christian story and its message, which is outlined in this book, conforms to this baseline of what God has arranged.

As we go on deeper into this story and message, we will find God's loving mercy provides opportunities to avoid these fates, for those who take advantage of them. However, in spite of God making an escape of the fates His Judgment has put in place, those who do not take advantage of this escape are doomed to go through everything outlined above—no exception. These judgments have sealed themselves to the human experience.

These additional opportunities of redemption will only help those who take advantage of them. For the rest, everything will stand as it is. If taken advantage of, individuals can avoid that which has been established—the coming day of judgment. More about this will be explained as we continue.

CHAPTER 2

The Great Dragon—that Ancient Serpent

Who is called the Devil or Satan (he who is the seducer and the deceiver of all humanity; the world over)...

Amp Revelation 12:9

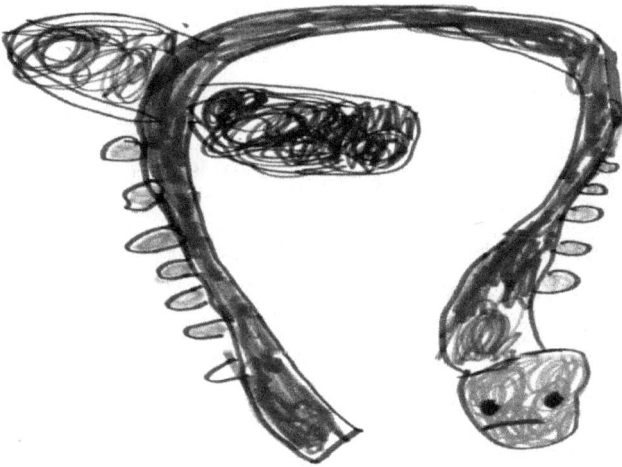

The story of man is tied to the story of the Devil, as we have seen in the fall. The Devil is a celestial being. His body is made up of supernatural matter, and not natural matter as that of man's. He is a spirit being, like an angel, and his natural habitat is in the spiritual realm where his body can function and be seen.

He was called the mighty angelic guardian who could walk among the fiery stones before the throne of God. This reflects a high status. However, he lost that status of the mighty angelic guardian of the garden. We heard that he had corrupted his wisdom on account of his great beauty—his vanity. He thinks more of himself than he is. This creature is blatantly in rebellion towards God; he wants to rule all things instead of God, and wants to lord over men. He wants for himself his own kingdom and God's Kingdom to rule over.

Since only God is creative and has creative power, the Devil cannot create something out of nothing as God can. As a result, he wants what is not his; otherwise, he would have no kingdom of his own. We know from the tree that he despises what God has given him and wants what God has not given him.

In other words, he wants what is outside his garden. He wants these things with a violence and hostility. He has a fierce jealousy and covetousness within him, and his spirit became the sole source of the spirit of covetousness. Jesus says he is a liar and the father of all lies. He invented them.

Since he lacks creative power, how does all this work for him? Simple. He discovered for himself that to be independent from God all he has to do is, first, disobey God. Second, hate what God gives him. Third, want only what God has not given him—to covet. Where does he get his power to struggle against God? Again, very elementary, he rebels against God by doing the opposite of God, and His commands. We know this is true because Paul said:

NIV 1Co 15:56 *The sting of death is sin, and the power of sin is the law.*

NIV Ro 4:15 *because law brings wrath. And where there is no law there is no transgression.*

It is so elementary. However, the Devil needs to wait for God to make a command. Then, the covetousness and rebellion of his spirit is stirred up according to his wisdom, and he has a power or an ability to rebel against God. He does so by not conforming and instead doing what the command says not to do. If God does not make a command, then the Devil has no ability to give expression to his covetousness and rebellion. It's like a dead seed that can remain in a dormant state for years. However, when mixed with soil and water, it becomes active, and out of it can grow a mighty tree.

This is why Paul said, "The power of sin is the law (1 Co 15:56)," and "Where there is no law, there is no transgression (Ro 4:15)." Without the law, rebellion and covetousness are invisible spirit qualities with nothing to oppose. It is then, therefore, a dormant and unexpressed spiritual energy. However, it is real, and it is a life-principle. It is a spirit force that is disharmonic and divisive, just hanging out there in the universe waiting for something, anything, to fuel and agitate its power, causing it to grow, bear fruit, and have expression.

It's like the old saying that goes, "It takes two to tango." Violence cannot be violent unless it has something to be violent against. Again, it's just an unexpressed life-principle—spirit energy. The fact that it is dormant does not make it less real or less of a threat to the harmony that it is divided against and opposes once finding its water and soil to grow in. It's like cancer that is dormant in the body. It is no less of a threat to the individual and only a matter of time before it finds a way to have expression and grow, doing its deadly work once it has what is required for it to come out of its dormancy.

Therefore, the spirit of the Devil (whose power comes from covetousness, lust, jealousy, and rebellion) lusts after and wants what is sinful so that its spirit power is fueled. It has as its motives not an actual desire for a particular thing; its desire is for what that thing represents.

What desiring or trying to attain that particular thing represents is what causes him to be divided from God. It uses all that is sinful and forbidden as a means to fuel and increase its power to separate itself from God and have whatever is outside of what God gives and allows. The Devil has declared everything outside of God as his kingdom. Covetousness is the way to attain it (to desire what God has not given you).

This is a most important concept! The spirit of the Devil has been corrupted, and by its corrupt wisdom, it has become the spirit of covetousness. He has a spirit which violently, fiercely, and holistically wants what is forbidden him. His spirit has the sole motive of growing stronger in becoming independent from God and, thus, a god unto himself.

As it was stated, wisdom is a faculty of the spirit and, as a result, operates outside of word knowledge and before words are formed in the mind to understand it. Wisdom is a set of values by which to perceive through. Wisdom is perspective, outlook, and attitude. The outlook of a spirit is unique to the spirit.

For example, the spirit of jealousy has as an outlook of anger that presumes that it is not fair that someone has something it doesn't. Whereas, the spirit of fear has as its outlook a dread that things are outside of its control. Each spirit has, as a result of its qualities, a unique outlook that allows the mind to understand a matter in a certain light and only within that light.

The corrupt wisdom of the Devil is to perceive everything as if he is god and the center of all things, resulting in an outlook which sees all things in a self-centered, self-serving, self-sustaining, controlling, and self-gratifying way. The same spirit of the Devil, whose world view is as such, is comprised of a life-principle (energy) that fiercely lusts after and covets the forbidden, with the motives of becoming independent of God.

It matters not what the object is that is forbidden to have. It makes no distinction. In order to grow and be nurtured, it needs something, anything, and consumes everything that is forbidden in order to do so. It's like food; what food do we like? We crave, desire, and have a taste for the very things that supply nutrition that our bodies hunger for in order to grow. Those taste good to us (whatever they may be).

What a wretched, evil, dark, and twisted spirit power (life-principle) within the Devil—a power by which he is aware of all things, sees all things, and gives expression to all things in light of becoming independent from God.

This is the fruit that Adam and Eve ingested and integrated into the human spirit. Like a dormant cancer within, just waiting for the right water and soil to infest the whole body is the fruit that they consumed into their spirit. This is how all children born of a woman since the beginning have been effected by what Adam and Eve did. This monstrous, God-hating life-principle passed onto us by Adam and Eve is what God holds against all people who possess the human spirit of Adam, even before it has a chance to fester within the individual soul.

Therefore, when it says Adam and Eve ingested the fruit of the tree of the knowledge of good and evil so they too could be like God, it is talking about the spirit of the Devil they took into their hearts with its qualities, motives, outlook, wisdom, and spirit life-principle (power). Sin is a life-principle, and therefore, sin is a spirit—it is the spirit of the Devil. In Genesis 3:3-5, the serpent created an unholy desire in Adam and Eve to have something that God didn't give them—a covetousness.

Here is the biggest lie of the Devil we operate out of: if you desire and lust for something you do not have, want something someone else has, or want something you are forbidden to have, it is the spirit of sin within you which wants it. More precisely, it is the spirit of the Devil adopted into the human spirit that covets for it. That spirit lays dormant within, infused with our human spirit, until it can fuel itself by latching onto a forbidden desire which will give it the soil and water it needs to grow and become inflamed with its expressed purpose to have opportunity to divide from God.

When the lust of covetousness stirs and agitates within us evil desires, we as humans believe it is because we really want a certain thing that is withheld from us. Like for example, the neighbor's wife. We think our desire is out of love. The desire is not love but the covetousness within.

Herein is the truth which exposes the lie. It is the spirit of sin, the spirit essence of the Devil within us, which seizes the opportunity of the forbidden being present (the water and soil) to carry out its objective. That motive and objective to be independent from God is what makes us feel like we are desperate to have the neighbor's wife. The desperation, lust, jealousy, and desire we experience towards her (that we interpret as love) is a lie.

What we feel towards her is not really a desire for her, but an inflamed power within to be rebellious and independent from God. What we are experiencing is the inflamed spirit of the Devil that is integrated within our human spirit. Truly, it is not desperate and hopeless love for the neighbor's wife that we are overwhelmed with that drives us uncontrollably to commit adultery. It is the power of the spirit of the Devil having opportunity to rage within us to have and take what is not ours. We mistake this feeling for love. That is the lie.

We as Christians often feel a desire to have something outside of our garden, causing us to beg God in our prayers to give us that which He has not ordained. We sometimes feel like it is unfair that when we want something, it is that very thing that we are being denied by God. "Why does God want to take away the thing that I like the most?" Or, "How come I am the only one I know who doesn't have one or can't afford one?" The whole concept is a lie, and it is pitiful that the majority of the Church is naive to it.

The sin nature, the spirit of covetousness within which Adam ingested and poisoned the human spirit with, only wants it so that it may be independent and divide from God. Covetous desires all take place in our very essence, in that place beyond words. We need to wake up and recognize the lie so we don't entertain and explore that which inflames the very thing inside of us that we, as Christians, are trying to kill. Not discerning what spirit our desires stem from can totally debilitate us from having union and being in harmony with God.

Keep in mind that sin is life-principle (spirit) which provides perception, motivation, inspiration, and the power to carry out an act, all of which make it a spirit force. This spirit force is the spirit of the Devil. Sin is the spirit of the Devil, because he is the originator of it and the fountain out of which this spirit power flows. Most importantly, it is sin that brings with it death. Understanding the spirit of sin with new glasses, we will now look at these difficult passages about the power of sin within that Paul writes about in Romans.

Amp Ro 7:5 When we were living in the flesh (mere physical lives), the sinful passions that were awakened and aroused up by [what] the Law [makes sin] were constantly operating in our natural powers (in our bodily organs, in the sensitive appetites and wills of the flesh), so that we bore fruit for death.

Amp Ro 7:7 What then do we conclude? Is the Law identical with sin? Certainly not! Nevertheless, if it had not been for the Law, I should not have recognized sin or have known its meaning. [For instance] I would not have known about covetousness [would have had no consciousness of sin or sense of guilt] if the Law had not [repeatedly] said, You shall not covet and have an evil desire [for one thing and another].

Amp Ro 7:8 But sin, *finding opportunity in the commandment [to express itself], got a hold on me and aroused and stimulated all kinds of forbidden desires (lust, covetousness). For without the Law sin is dead [the sense of it is inactive and a lifeless thing].*

Amp Ro 7:9 Once I was alive, but quite apart from and unconscious of the Law. But when the commandment came, sin lived again and I died (was sentenced by the Law to death).

Amp Ro 7:10 And the very legal ordinance which was designed and intended to bring life actually proved [to mean to me] death.

Amp Ro 7:11 For sin, seizing the opportunity and getting a hold on me [by taking its incentive] from the commandment, beguiled and entrapped and cheated me, and using it [as a weapon], killed me.

Amp Ro 7:12 The Law therefore is holy, and [each] commandment is holy and just and good.

Amp Ro 7:13 Did that which is good then prove fatal [bringing death] to me? Certainly not! It was sin, working death in me by using this good thing [as a weapon], in order that through the commandment sin might be shown up clearly to be sin, that the extreme malignity and immeasurable sinfulness of sin might plainly appear.

Amp Ro 7:14 We know that the Law is spiritual; but I am a creature of the flesh [carnal, unspiritual], having been sold into slavery under [the control of] sin.

Amp Ro 7:15 For I do not understand my own actions [I am baffled, bewildered]. I do not practice or accomplish what I wish, but I do the very thing that I loathe [which my moral instinct condemns].

Amp Ro 7:16 Now if I do [habitually] what is contrary to my desire, [that means that] I acknowledge and agree that the Law is good (morally excellent) and that I take sides with it.

Amp Ro 7:17 However, it is no longer I who do the deed, but the sin [principle] which is at home in me and has possession of me.

Amp Ro 7:18 For I know that nothing good dwells within me, that is, in my flesh. I can will what is right, but I cannot perform it. [I have the intention and urge to do what is right, but no power to carry it out.]

Amp Ro 7:19 For I fail to practice the good deeds I desire to do, but the evil deeds that I do not desire to do are what I am [ever] doing.

Amp Ro 7:20 Now if I do what I do not desire to do, it is no longer I doing it [it is not myself that acts], but the sin [principle] which dwells within me [fixed and operating in my soul].

Amp Ro 7:21 So I find it to be a law (rule of action of my being) that when I want to do what is right and good, evil is ever present with me and I am subject to its insistent demands.

Amp Ro 7:22 For I endorse and delight in the Law of God in my inmost self [with my new nature].

Amp Ro 7:23 But I discern in my bodily members [in the sensitive appetites and wills of the flesh] a different law (rule of action) at war against the law of my mind (my reason) and making me a prisoner to the law of sin that dwells in my bodily organs [in the sensitive appetites and wills of the flesh].

Amp Ro 7:24 O unhappy and pitiable and wretched man that I am! Who will release and deliver me from [the shackles of] this body of death?

Amp Ro 7:25 O thank God! [He will!] through Jesus Christ (the Anointed One) our Lord! So then indeed I, of myself with the mind and heart, serve the Law of God, but with the flesh the law of sin.

Amp Ro 8:1 THEREFORE, [there is] now no condemnation (no adjudging guilty of wrong) for those who are in Christ Jesus, who live [and] walk not after the dictates of the flesh, but after the dictates of the Spirit.

Amp Ro 8:2 For the law of the Spirit of life [which is] in Christ Jesus [the law of our new being] has freed me from the law of sin and of death.

Amp Ro 8:3 For God has done what the Law could not do, [its power] being weakened by the flesh [the entire nature of man without the Holy Spirit]. Sending His own Son in the guise of sinful flesh and as an offering for sin, [God] condemned sin in the flesh [subdued, overcame, deprived it of its power over all who accept that sacrifice],

Amp Ro 8:4 So that the righteous and just requirement of the Law might be fully met in us who live and move not in the ways of the flesh but in the ways of the Spirit [our lives governed not by the standards and according to the dictates of the flesh, but controlled by the Holy Spirit].

Amp Ro 8:5 For those who are according to the flesh and are controlled by its unholy desires set their minds on and pursue those things which gratify the flesh, but those who are according to the Spirit and are controlled by the desires of the Spirit set their minds on and seek those things which gratify the [Holy] Spirit.

Amp Ro 8:6 Now the mind of the flesh [which is sense and reason without the Holy Spirit] is death [death that comprises all the miseries arising from sin, both here and hereafter]. But the mind of the [Holy] Spirit is life and [soul] peace [both now and forever].

Amp Ro 8:7 [That is] because the mind of the flesh [with its carnal thoughts and purposes] is hostile to God, for it does not submit itself to God's Law; indeed it cannot.

Amp Ro 8:8 So then those who are living the life of the flesh [catering to the appetites and impulses of their carnal nature] cannot please or satisfy God, or be acceptable to Him.

Amp Ro 8:9 But you are not living the life of the flesh, you are living the life of the Spirit, if the [Holy] Spirit of God [really] dwells within you [directs and controls you]. But if anyone does not possess the [Holy] Spirit of Christ, he is none of His [he does not belong to Christ, is not truly a child of God].

Amp Ro 8:10 But if Christ lives in you, [then although] your [natural] body is dead by reason of sin and guilt, the spirit is alive because of [the] righteousness [that He imputes to you].

Amp Ro 8:11 And if the Spirit of Him Who raised up Jesus from the dead dwells in you, [then] He Who raised up Christ Jesus from the dead will also restore to life your mortal (short-lived, perishable) bodies through His Spirit Who dwells in you.

Amp Ro 7:6 But now we are discharged from the Law and have terminated all intercourse with it, having died to what once restrained and held us captive. So now we serve not under [obedience to] the old code of written regulations, but [under obedience to the promptings] of the Spirit in newness [of life].

CHAPTER 3

The Religion of Cain

Below is an excerpt from the book, *Christianity, A Lost Civilization*, by the same authors:

To pick a compromising idea in the contemporary Church and expound on it for the sake of looking at the religion of Cain, we will look at the example of homosexuality in the Church. There is a growing movement in Church leadership circles to search the Bible in an effort to justify homosexuality as acceptable. This movement thinks of their peers who believe it to be sin as being archaic and close-minded. They think it is a social duty and sign of progressive intelligence that one should find within the Scriptures, verses that can be interpreted to accept and support homosexuality. After all, all of society is moving towards accepting homosexuals as natural, and they don't want to see the Church left behind when it comes to [adapting to] these new social morals. The tables have almost been completely turned, and, according to society, the one who is not acceptable is the one who views homosexuality as unacceptable. They are labeled as homophobic. What needs to be recognized is that there is a great prejudice and persecution developing against those who do not deem homosexuality as wholesome.

We have always pointed out that there are three types of homosexuals. The first group have a hard heart towards God. They really don't care about His precepts, and simply want to indulge their own pleasures, not caring about the right or wrong of it.

The second group of homosexuals are like every other group of people who sin and are outside of the will of God as put forth in the Bible. The Bible is not unclear in viewing homosexuality as an abominable sin in the eyes of God. The Bible says, if you have broken one law you have broken them all. Accordingly, in our understanding, the homosexual is not looked at any different than the adulterer, or the thief, or the murderer, and so on. They see their former activity as a sin—something they need to repent of, seek forgiveness for from God, and to refrain from, as all sinners do. If they stumble, it is treated like any other sin someone else might stumble in. They repent, ask forgiveness and renew their efforts to not indulge in that sin anymore. This group is welcomed like any other sinner who wants to restore fellowship with God.

However, the third type of homosexual defiantly says, "God must forgive me and accept me for who I am." And "I can't love a God who doesn't love me the way I am." "He isn't a forgiving God if He can't accept me as is." One needs to ask why this sin should be treated differently than any other sin, and why it does not need to be refrained from as other sins do.

In this post-modern Church world, it is the non-Christians, the ones who are in nonconformity to God and neither practice the ways of the Bible nor are educated in the ways of the Bible, who are dictating to the Christians what is right and wrong about how they embrace their faith. They insist that Christianity should co-exist with others without judging them as in sin. They blame the Christian's reluctance to agree with them as the root cause of disunity, prejudice, and all violence in the world. Many influential modern Christian thinkers see wisdom in this thinking. As a result, they work towards trying to conform Christian beliefs and Biblical understandings to the non-Christian way of thinking and its moralities (which are to give acceptance [even salvation] without conformity to God and His precepts).

These notions make following the Bible archaic, crude, and barbaric. Again, the thinking is, to have such archaic ideas as put forth in the Bible fosters prejudice and disunity, leading to violence against those who are deemed unacceptable. Therefore, this makes imposing Biblical values the cause of all violence, prejudice, and disunity in the world. Supposed progressive Christian thinkers and leaders who accept this view see a huge need to re-evaluate Christian values in a way that brings acceptance and unity to the rest of the world who are not in fellowship with God (as Christians know Him).

Where this leads them is to a place where they have to accept the moral and religious values that exist in the world as merely a belief system that people live by. Meaning, we Christians have to accept that what the Muslims believe and what the Koran says is truth to them, and we have no business challenging that truth when it is in opposition to ours, but must accept it as truth for them. What this does, in essence, is make all belief systems vain and impotent. They are not reality; one is not right over the other, but all are just a set of beliefs that have their own logic.

Truth is then subjective, and other truths are just as valid as Christian truth. By this thinking, Christianity is therefore reduced to just a concept by which one can understand themselves through. It is not right, it is not wrong, it is not a true reality which is absolute. The only thing that makes it true is because (1) somebody is willing to believe it as true and (2) it has a logic of its own just as other veins of logic make sense to others. We should therefore understand that everybody else's religion is just as true as ours, and we should not deem them as in error, even if their religion is in conflict with ours. Christianity is reduced to a mythology so that we do not judge others according to its values.

As a side note, other religions such as Islam, for example, do not share this generous idealism. They believe their truth is absolute, and Christianity is in error. They believe that for us to co-exist with them we need to accept their beliefs and deny our own. This holds true even with the homosexual contingency. The homosexual community believes their ideals—to do what one wills and for all to accept them (including God)—to be an absolute truth, and Christian thinking to be in error. However, in reality, their way, is the way of Cain.

This attitude towards God is not unique to homosexuality, however, homosexuality is the end times catalyst for this type of movement (acceptance without conformity—the way of Cain). This movement will overtake the world, even within major elements of the Church. As the truth of this epidemic is exposed, it will create nothing short of a civil war within the Church. This is God's judgment against the Church, a judgment which has been set in stone. The die has already been cast, the gavel has gone down, and the Church of Christ will soon be torn in two. The pity of it all is that the *Church Pure* will be the powerless minority.

Let us look at a couple of verses in the Bible which address this subject, including one of the first stories in the Bible where non-conformity to God is recorded, and see how this lines up with the premise that Christian Biblical values are the root cause which fosters prejudice, division, and violence in the world.

Cain and Abel

NIV Ge 4:1 Adam lay with his wife Eve, and she became pregnant and gave birth to Cain. She said, "With the help of the LORD I have brought forth a man."

NIV Ge 4:2 Later she gave birth to his brother Abel. Now Abel kept flocks, and Cain worked the soil.

NIV Ge 4:3 In the course of time Cain brought some of the fruits of the soil as an offering to the LORD.

NIV NIV Ge 4:4 But Abel brought fat portions from some of the firstborn of his flock. The LORD looked with favor on Abel and his offering,

NIV NIV Ge 4:5 but on Cain and his offering he did not look with favor. So Cain was very angry, and his face was downcast.

NIV Ge 4:6 Then the LORD said to Cain, "Why are you angry? Why is your face downcast?

NIV Ge 4:7 If you do what is right, will you not be accepted? But if you do not do what is right, sin is crouching at your door; it desires to have you, but you must master it."

NIV NIV Ge 4:8 Now Cain said to his brother Abel, "Let's go out to the field." And while they were in the field, Cain attacked his brother Abel and killed him.

NIV Ge 4:9 Then the LORD said to Cain, "Where is your brother Abel?" "I don't know, " he replied. "Am I my brother's keeper?"

NIV Ge 4:10 The LORD said, "What have you done? Listen! Your brother's blood cries out to me from the ground.

NIV Ge 4:11 Now you are under a curse and driven from the ground, which opened its mouth to receive your brother's blood from your hand.

NIV Ge 4:12 When you work the ground, it will no longer yield its crops for you. You will be a restless wanderer on the earth."

NIV Ge 4:13 Cain said to the LORD, "My punishment is more than I can bear.

$^{NIV\ Ge\ 4:14}$ Today you are driving me from the land, and I will be hidden from your presence; I will be a restless wanderer on the earth, and whoever finds me will kill me."

$^{NIV\ Ge\ 4:15}$ But the LORD said to him, "Not so ;if anyone kills Cain, he will suffer vengeance seven times over." Then the LORD put a mark on Cain so that no one who found him would kill him.

$^{NIV\ Ge\ 4:16}$ So Cain went out from the LORD'S presence and lived in the land of Nod, east of Eden.

$^{NIV\ Ge\ 4:17}$ Cain lay with his wife, and she became pregnant and gave birth to Enoch. Cain was then building a city, and he named it after his son Enoch.

Let's look at how this story applies to what we have been discussing above. The verses above infer that God demanded a certain prescribed form of worship from the people who were alive at that time. It's pretty clear that God accepted Abel's offering and was pleased with it, however, the offering that Cain brought to Him was not acceptable or in line with what God demanded. This put him in disunity with God. Perhaps God wanted an animal sacrifice which was of more value to the worshiper, and Cain decided to give Him vegetables as a sacrifice, since, in his way of thinking, that is what he had an abundance of since he worked the ground. Perhaps he did not want to give up one of the few sheep that he had. We will see later that Jude referred to this as "the way of Cain." However, for our purposes, we like to refer to these circumstances as "the religion of Cain." After all, this all surrounds issues in worshiping or relating to God in an acceptable manner, which would be according to His own will.

Because Cain did not do what was acceptable to the one he made an offering to, God was not pleased and did not accept his offering. We are told Cain got jealous of his brother's acceptance with God, and it angered him that what he decided to offer was not accepted. Cain took as a personal affront the fact that his brother's deeds earned him acceptance and that his did not. His brother Abel's deeds were not at all pointed towards Cain nor were they meant to be a statement about Cain. They were simply deeds that were meant to honor God, irrespective of his feelings towards Cain.

In other words, this was a problem between Cain and God. However, Cain didn't see it that way; he saw his brother's acceptance with God as a personal affront or a statement against him, and therefore saw his brother as a threat to his relationship with God. So he eliminated that threat. It's like saying, "God should be happy with how I decide to honor Him." It's kind of like giving your wife a 500 piece craftsmen socket set as a gift for her birthday and then wondering, "why is she so upset?"

Many years back, when one of my sons was young and in grade school, perhaps the 1st grade, he hated having to be in school. As a result, he showed his protest by not really doing all of the work demanded of him. One day, we got a communication from his teacher stating she wanted to place him in special education because he wasn't learning or absorbing anything. This shocked us because he was an intelligent boy. She gave us the example of how there were some 30 words that his classmates understood how to spell, and my son retained none of them and, as a result, was several months behind the rest of the students when it came to reading. They were reading and he was not.

She went on to tell me what a sweet boy he was and perhaps he was inapt to grasp what was being taught. Then she told me how just a day ago she had given the class a test, and when it was over my son handed in the test without answering any of the questions. Instead, he drew a pretty picture of a flower for the teacher. She said she did not know how to handle this because he was so sweet about it, but for whatever reasons, he is not adapting to the work.

When I hung up with her I asked my son, "Why did you give the teacher a flower instead of doing the work she asked of you?" He told me it was because he didn't want to do the work asked of him, and he didn't want to be in school. He figured he would just do something nice for her since he didn't want to do the work. When we got upset with him for not doing the work, he got his feelings crushed and wondered why we were so upset when he did such a nice thing for the teacher by drawing her a flower. Of course this defiance made him not acceptable among his peers and almost cost him a huge setback in his education.

The way the story ended was I had gotten a list of those 30 words that night while on the phone with the teacher. I made flashcards with them and spent about 2 hours making him say the words, then spell the words, and then say the words once again. I did this repeatedly, recycling through the words over again until he could say it, spell it, say it without making a single mistake on all 30 words. It started out as something he refused to do and claimed he didn't know what the words were. He kept pleading with me and crying while saying things like, "I can't," I don't know how," "I don't know what they mean," and "I can't remember." It was as if he was being willfully and defiantly stupid.

That ended when he finally understood that I was unwilling to relent and we were not going to stop doing these flashcards until he knew them all without mistakes. However, it ended in an amazing way. He finally got into the spirit, made an effort, and stopped resisting what he was supposed to do. He became so enthusiastic once he made this switch, that he sat down and wrote letters to 4 or 5 family members now that he could write and spell words. In addition, in his own excitement of what he had learned, he read all of the storybooks he had received from school, which were used to teach him how to read. Through forcing him to no longer be defiant (doing what he pleased, and stubbornly not conforming to his authority), I turned around his situation at school in one evening. He was several months behind, and after one evening, he went back to school excelling past the other students. His teacher was astonished and quite pleased and there was no more talk about putting him in special education.

It seems God took the same stance with Cain. He said, "Why are you angry?" "If you do what is right, will you not be accepted?" In other words, he was saying to Cain, "I'm God and you are not; I'm in charge and you are not; I lead, you follow; I'm the one who decides what is right and acceptable, you don't tell me. So why are you angry that your deeds were not acceptable to me? Why are you jealous that your brother received acceptance when he did what was demanded? There is nothing to be upset about, I am not mad at you, all you have to do is what is acceptable. Then you will be accepted—problem solved!"

However, unlike my son and instead like many of the people I have had conversations with when it comes to getting right with God, this was not (in their thinking) an acceptable way of remedying the situation for Cain. Like the many people I have talked to, Cain decided he didn't think it was fair that God did not accept him. He thought that God should be happy with the way he honored Him. "I can't love a God who won't be happy with how I decide to honor Him." "

If He can't accept my way, then I don't want Him, after all I'm trying to do something nice for Him." When I hear these kinds of comments from people, I cringe in fear, wondering if they really understand what is at stake by being so defiant and asking the God of the entire universe—their Maker—to accept them under their terms and not His.

What we can ascertain from this story is that the religion of Cain is a religion that tells God, "You have to accept me on my terms, and You have to be happy with how I choose to honor You, or I will not accept

You at all." Furthermore, the story shows us that God does not allow acceptance without conformity—the opposite of what the religion of Cain demands. We see as a result of this it was Cain that put himself outside of fellowship with God by his own choice, and estranged himself from all who do as God demands and, therefore, are accepted. What disunited Cain from God and his fellow man was not, in fact, prejudice on their part. He was not pushed on the outside, but he distinguished himself as separate and not in agreement/harmony with all who are willing to conform. It was his defiance and nonconformity to what is right in the eyes of God that isolated him from those who do conform.

Another important point of this story is that it is not the prejudice of those who do conform that fostered violence. No violence was perpetrated on Cain. He was merely dis-fellowshipped by his own refusal to be as others were. Cain refused to conform, but demanded to be accepted. When he did not get acceptance without conformity, it was he who became so enraged in his jealousy, contempt, and defiance, that he was the one who committed violence; even the first murder. What this means is that the opposite is true, nonconformity to God fosters violence.

According to the first occasion of someone not yielding to God's will, demanding acceptance without conformity: prejudice, disunity, hatred, violence and murder comes from them—the nonconformist. Violence is born out of their nonconformity. Hatred and violence do not come from those who hold fast to God's laws.

The righteous may judge others who do not conform to God's laws, viewing their standing as unacceptable. However, when they do so, it is not because of their own personal judgment, but because of the laws God has made, which the righteous adhere to. The conformers and their views are not to blame for all the prejudice and violence in the world. These things come from those who defy God's laws, demand acceptance without conformity, and are determined to have whatever they desire at any cost.

This is the true root of all we face in today's world, which the great thinkers are trying to solve. Alas, God Himself already solved the problem, and told us the solution, making it simple, and putting the burden where it belongs—on the defiant ones. That solution is: "If you do what is right, will you not be accepted?" The Lord puts the solution in the form of a question so we stop and think, "Of course! What was I thinking?" To undo what was done that caused disunity, will make everything right.

At this point, the homosexual nonconformist will point out that there are Christian organizations such as the KKK and other Christian white supremacist groups who do perpetrate violence on the outcasts who do not believe the same things as they do. All we would say in answer to this is that these extremist groups do not conform to the true Spirit of Christ any more than the homosexual contingency we are referring to. Therefore, it wouldn't be fair to judge Christians who truly conform to God by the standards of those who do not, any more than it would be right to judge the standards of the Christian Church by those whose standards acknowledge homosexuality as an acceptable Christian practice.

As in the case of Cain, the gay Christians who insist that God should accept them the way they are stubbornly will not relent in their non-conformity. And as this is the case, the only thing left to give if there is to be acceptance (in their way of thinking) is for God and the Christians to give them acceptance without conformity. Since they do not get acceptance, they project onto those in harmony with God that they are to blame why they do not have it, just as Cain projected onto his brother Abel. However, what Abel did was not a statement against Cain but an act to honor God. It is the same for those who uphold the laws of God in the area of sexuality in relationship with those who do not but demand acceptance. For true unity and acceptance, we all need to line up with the will of God. Likewise, the Church leaders should also wake up and see that they are mistaken to buy into the point of view of those who refuse to conform, and, therefore, they should stop giving religious acceptance without conformity for (in their minds) the sake of harmony. Their mistaken ideas have the opposite effect and promote anarchy, lawlessness, and disorder.

Below, Jude shows he knows the truth of the story of Cain—his religious ways of relating to God and to his fellow man. Listen to how he speaks of those who insist on having the religion of Cain and the leaders who agree with their point of view. Included in this group Jude is addressing are those who would turn the Church of God into a market place, finding a way to peddle God's salvation for profit to feed themselves. Shame on those who trifle with the salvation God made as a free gift for man, and interpreting it in ways which enrich them. For salvation does not come from man that he can make it mean what he wants it to mean and include who he wants it to include. No, salvation is from God and it is for those He designed it for.

NIV Jude 1:10 *Yet these men speak abusively against whatever they do not understand; and what things they do understand by instinct, like unreasoning animals—these are the very things that destroy them.*
NIV Jude 1:11 *Woe to them! They have taken the way of Cain; they have rushed for profit into Balaam's error; they have been destroyed in Korah's rebellion.*
NIV Jude 1:12 *These men are blemishes at your love feasts, eating with you without the slightest qualm—shepherds who feed only themselves. They are clouds without rain, blown along by the wind; autumn trees, without fruit and uprooted —twice dead.*
NIV Jude 1:13 *They are wild waves of the sea, foaming up their shame; wandering stars, for whom blackest darkness has been reserved forever.*
NIV Jude 1:14 *Enoch, the seventh from Adam, prophesied about these men: "See, the Lord is coming with thousands upon thousands of his holy ones*
NIV Jude 1:15 *to judge everyone, and to convict all the ungodly of all the ungodly acts they have done in the ungodly way, and of all the harsh words ungodly sinners have spoken against him."*
NIV Jude 1:16 *These men are grumblers and faultfinders; they follow their own evil desires; they boast about themselves and flatter others for their own advantage.[1]*

The error of Adam corrupted the human spirit in a way that brought an independence from God and a spirit power to divide from Him. This, thereby, causing humans to seek after that which is beyond what God wills and ordains for them. It also causes a person to perceive himself as the center of all things, with everything revolving around him. A desire and spirit perception to be independent from God brought death into the world. To bring true separation from our source of life is to bring death.

The error of the religion of Cain turns his rebellion back towards God, trying to force God to give acceptance without conformity and, in turn, do as he wills. It never sees as a solution for reconciliation with God to do what is right in His eyes. He deems the consequences of nonconformity as too harsh, even a perpetrated violence against him—he becomes the "victim." The religion of Cain sees only one solution: for God to accept him as he is. Therefore, he is unable to master rebellion and defiance; rather he comes under the bondage of it as does everyone who has the religion of Cain.

NIV Ge 4:7 *If you do what is right, will you not be accepted? But if you do not do what is right, sin is crouching at your door; it desires to have you, but you must master it."*

First, it was established that, through Adam, death entered into the world. Next, it will be shown how the religion of Cain brought anarchy and led to the judgment of water which caused the flood. After that, the third and final major step of the rebellion of man will be revealed. The origin of this rebellion is commonly overlooked. Nevertheless, it's importance is that it caused the third and final judgment against man—the judgment which brings the end of the world, and the destruction of the universe through fire instead of water.

Notes

[1] Livingston, P., & Livingston, C. (2015). *Christianity: A Lost Civilization.* Wauconda: The Naked Apostles.

CHAPTER 4

The Flood

^{Amp Ge 6:1} WHEN MEN began to multiply on the face of the land and daughters were born to them,

^{Amp Ge 6:2} The sons of God saw that the daughters of men were fair, and they took wives of all they desired and chose.

^{Amp Ge 6:3} Then the Lord said, My Spirit shall not forever dwell and strive with man, for he also is flesh; but his days shall yet be 120 years.

^{Amp Ge 6:4} There were giants on the earth in those days—and also afterward—when the sons of God lived with the daughters of men, and they bore children to them. These were the mighty men who were of old, men of renown.

^{Amp Ge 6:5} The Lord saw that the wickedness of man was great in the earth, and that every imagination and intention of all human thinking was only evil continually.

Amp Ge 6:6 And the Lord regretted that He had made man on the earth, and He was grieved at heart.

Amp Ge 6:7 So the Lord said, I will destroy, blot out, and wipe away mankind, whom I have created from the face of the ground—not only man, [but] the beasts and the creeping things and the birds of the air—for it grieves Me and makes Me regretful that I have made them.

Amp Ge 6:8 But Noah found grace (favor) in the eyes of the Lord.

The flood, you could say, is the second judgment against man. The first was in the garden when, through Adam, death entered into the world, among some other curses. Every person born of a woman had/has a death sentence hanging over them, even while in the womb. No one has escaped death. At this point in history, the heart of God is so pained that He is sorry He created man, and He has judged that waiting for the natural course of the world to run out and for all men to die is too much to bear. So He decides to destroy man and wipe him from the face of the earth in one fell swoop through a global flood. Only one family is to survive, Noah and his family.

What was so bad that this should be the case? We are told in the verses immediately above why He decided to destroy humankind.

Amp Ge 6:2 The sons of God saw that the daughters of men were fair, and they took wives of all they desired and chose.

Amp Ge 6:3 Then the Lord said, My Spirit shall not forever dwell and strive with man, for he also is flesh; but his days shall yet be 120 years.

Amp Ge 6:4 There were giants on the earth in those days—and also afterward—when the sons of God lived with the daughters of men, and they bore children to them. These were the mighty men who were of old, men of renown.

The sons of God these verses are referring to are angels, in fact, fallen angels. Giants (the Nephilim), the mighty men who were of old, men of renown: these names are referring to the same group of people. They were the resulting offspring of angels from the supernatural realm who possessed celestial bodies crossbreeding with women of the natural realm with physical bodies. The resulting offspring were these giants called Nephilim.

Every mythology around the globe speaks of both the fallen angels who spawn them and the giants they fathered. The fallen angels were referred to as gods, for example, Zeus and Thetis. Their half-supernatural, half-natural children were demigods, for example, Hercules the son of Zeus and Achilles the son of Thetis. The Bible is calling men like Hercules and Achilles giants, mighty men of renown. When they use the name, "mighty men," they mean mighty warriors as well as giants.

Nimrod, grandson of Cush, the Bible refers to as one of these mighty men. Indeed, Nimrod was a mighty warrior. It was said that no one could win a fight with him. It has also been recorded that he was over 11 feet tall. Another famous Biblical giant/mighty warrior was Goliath, whom David defeated in battle.

There is a popular school of thought that holds the belief that the sons of God were not in fact angels, but the sons of Seth, who were godly in nature, unlike the sons of Cain. The main thinking is that the Bible tells us that angels do not propagate and, furthermore, they are neither male nor female. In addition to that, they are supernatural creatures whose bodies are of supernatural matter, unlike the natural man whose body is made of natural matter.

However true these facts are, there obviously was a way in which this was able to happen. It is the perversion of these two realms coming together, the natural and the supernatural, that made the earth a place like hell to live on, causing something so drastic as the flood. Peter and Jude disagree with that school of thought. In fact, the Bible agrees that these sons of God were actually angels and not just godly men, the sons of Seth.

Peter not only agrees that these were angels and not men, but he ties these disobedient angels to the ungodly men, who together brought on the cause for the flood. Below is a verse from 2 Peter that makes reference to these fallen angels and their fate.

NAS 2PE 2:4 For if God did not spare angels when they sinned, but cast them into hell and committed them to pits of darkness, reserved for judgment;
NAS 2PE 2:5 and did not spare the ancient world, but preserved Noah, a preacher of righteousness, with seven others, when He brought a flood upon the world of the ungodly . . .

Things were so bad on the earth that angels mixed their DNA with almost all types of living things in the natural world. This is why in mythology there are abortions of nature such as half-animals and half-men, like the minotaurs, centaurs, and even perhaps mermaids. These are mythical creatures and it is difficult to think of them as anything but legend, however, they are mentioned in the book of Jashar. Jashar is an apocrypha book. Jashar is a sacred Hebrew text and is mentioned in the Bible twice as an affirmation of those events that are recorded in the Bible ("Is not this written in the book of Jashar." It reads in Joshua 10:13 and again in 2 Samuel giving credence to another event).

Amp Ge 6:7 So the Lord said, I will destroy, blot out, and wipe away mankind, whom I have created from the face of the ground—not only man, [but] the beasts and the creeping things and the birds of the air

It is not that we support belief in the mythologies of the world, because we do not, however, it would be remiss to ignore supporting evidence that gives witness to the Bible. Why is it wrong to embrace the Bible as canon and the truth from God, and then use (while holding loosely) the recorded history of the world as a witness and aid in understanding what the Bible tells us? Even to use recorded history to fill in a few Biblical pictures?

It is part of our faith to embrace the Bible as truth and our source of truth, measuring all things according to its standards. Likewise, according to our faith, it would be wrong to believe other recorded documents above the truths written in the Bible or to think there is any other saving knowledge needed for man outside the contents of the Bible.

However, it is a ridiculous notion to believe that this means we give no credence to any other writings, nor do we trust any other document or strictly make reference to the Bible only, making it a sin to read or believe any other document in history. In fact, there are 22 books that are mentioned in the Bible as references by the authors of the Bible. For example, Jude makes reference to the book of Enoch.

In order to see how Biblical truths are reflected in cultures around the world, here is an example of two Chinese characters of their written language: The Chinese character for "to covet" has the woman symbol combined with two trees. That would be Eve and the tree of life and the tree of the knowledge of good and evil. The Chinese character for a boat combines vessel with a person, and the number 8. There were 8 persons in Noah's ark.[2]

In almost every culture on earth there are references to the flood, just as there are to gods and demigods. Most of the mythologies around the world have close to the same stories as each other, their biggest differences being cultural settings and names that are in line with each language. The records and stories of myth are told from the perspective of the men who were subject to these gods and demigods as well as the perspective of the gods and demigods themselves. Beings who were dishonest, greedy, and fallen angels. On the other hand, our Biblical truths are written from the perspective of God, the Creator of heaven and earth, who is Truth. This distinguishes the one from the others.

Nevertheless, these stories in mythology have a basis in truth and in history. For example, in the letter from Jesus to the church of Pergamum found in Revelation, Jesus refers to Zeus, the king of the gods in Greek mythology, as Satan himself. The temple that holds the altar of Zeus Jesus is calling the throne of Satan, and its location in the city of Pergamum as the home of Satan. The temple and altar of Zeus built in Pergamum still can be seen today, and it is considered one of the wonders of the world. It was excavated and rebuilt in a museum in Germany.

The fallen angel Satan, the Devil, the father of all lies, and the cause of the fall of man, was known to the Greeks as the king of gods. Therefore, their gods are real. However, in reality, they are fallen angels in rebellion to God Almighty and not the heroes of mankind. The mythologies of the world are not the worshiping of lifeless idols (as some do) but the worship of fallen angels in rebellion towards God Almighty. Angels whose activities in the earth with men were such abominations to God that He wiped out mankind in a global flood. In addition, He incarcerated many of these angels in solitary pits in the deepest parts of the Abyss. Both men and the fallen angels they worshiped are being held over for the last day of judgment and the lake of fire.

NIV Rev 2:13 I know where you live—where Satan has his throne. Yet you remain true to my name. You did not renounce your faith in me, even in the days of Antipas, my faithful witness, who was put to death in your city—where Satan lives.

There are thousands of surviving ancient clay tablets from Babylon and Assyria, some of which predate the flood. Much of their content supports what the Bible teaches us. These documents often agree with Biblical accounts despite glorifying what the Bible calls evil. These recorded accounts of mythology are speaking about real figures in history and, thereby, witness to the truths of the Bible. That is, in spite of the fact that people worshipped these false gods before and after the flood and they were deceived not knowing who they really were, misinterpreting their exploits in the light of truth.

The reason that we include some extra Biblical accounts here is to help emphasize how dark, perverted, chaotic, and fearful it was in the days just before the flood. One has to consider the possibility that the dinosaurs, which were monstrous in size, like the human giants whose DNA were mixed with that of fallen angels, were actually abortions of nature due to what took place before the flood and were never meant to be.

These fallen angels and their offspring, the giants, have been recorded as teaching natural men:

- magic arts
- war and mass destruction
- women the art of seduction through making enticing clothing and applying make-up
- mysterious secrets of the supernatural realm which gave men powers over angels
- music and musical instruments which glorified the fallen angels and stirred the heart with a spirit to do as you will for pleasure (the same as the sex, drugs, and rock and roll spirit behind music today)

These are the kinds of things that specifically went on in the city that Cain built. Men either lived in mortal fear, appeasing/worshiping these fallen angels and the giants they spawned as a means to survive, or they empowered themselves with them, in their lust to conquest and attain superhuman powers.

Almost all lineage and DNA were corrupted and turned away from God while ruled by these fallen angels, except for that of Noah. God had good reason for bringing that world to an end, and also for incarcerating those fallen angels in the darkest pits of hell, holding them over for the lake of fire on the day of judgment—the last day.

Here is one final story to show how extra Biblical writings can help bring a clarity to the stories in the Bible:

Peter tied the fallen angels who mixed their DNA with humans to the cause of the flood. In the same way, Jude related the reason for the judgment against Sodom and Gomorrah to the judgment which brought on the flood. That reason was to crossbreed humans with angels. Jude does this to show that both cases are guilty of the same atrocities. However, the first case brought about the second judgment of the flood (water). Then, the second case of the same atrocities in the post-flood world brought about the third judgment of fire. This makes Sodom and Gomorrah a foretaste of the judgment of fire to come on the whole world because it was destroyed with fire and sulfur (brimstone). Jude was trying to help us see this so we don't just pass off the cause of the flood as legend, but use it to consider a serious change of heart. Jesus, too, said that in the end times it will be just as it was in the (pre-flood) days of Noah.

NAS JUDE 1:6 And angels who did not keep their own domain, but abandoned their proper abode, He has kept in eternal bonds under darkness for the judgment of the great day,
NAS JUDE 1:7 just as Sodom and Gomorrah and the cities around them, since they in the same way as these indulged in gross immorality and went after strange flesh, are exhibited as an example in undergoing the punishment of eternal fire.
NAS JUDE 1:8 Yet in the same way these men, also by dreaming, defile the flesh, and reject authority, and revile angelic majesties.

Now, as the story goes in the Bible, two angels stood in the town square until they were offered hospitality in the home of Lot (Abraham's nephew). This was a normal custom since there were no hotels for travelers. It was also a practice Abraham started, that was to give hospitality to travelers. After having done so, all the men of the cities of Sodom and Gomorrah, including all the surrounding towns of those city/states, gathered together and went to Lot's home, seeking out these two travelers.

It has been the popular thought that these men of all these cities and towns found out that there were travelers in town at Lot's house and they all gathered for the purpose to go have homosexual sex with them. The thinking is that their desire for homosexual sex brought the judgment of fire upon themselves and their cities and towns. As a result of this interpretation, anal sex has been referred to as sodomy, even in the laws of our country. This interpretation is bizarre, to say the least!

First of all, it is difficult to wrap one's mind around the idea that the news spread within hours to two cities and a handful of surrounding towns, for the sole purpose of informing the men that there were two unfamiliar travelers in town which could be used as sexual objects. Furthermore, to believe that all the male citizens from multiple towns had been waiting in anticipation, prepared to act at a moment's notice, when an opportunity to have a sexual encounter with complete strangers presented itself. As if travelers from another land were a rarity?

Secondly, that all the men of these cities and towns had a club which engaged in homosexuality. Furthermore, in their lust, they wanted someone different to engage in homosexual sex with? Why? They all were tired of having sex with each other (the entire population of men in two cities and some surrounding towns) and wanted someone new? As if they all had relations with each other in all the towns and were bored with the same old, same old? Or, that they all had a meeting, and all of the men in all the surrounding towns voted to go together as a community to Lot's house for the sole reason to pleasure themselves? And as a result same gender sex, and anal sex, is named after them?

It is in extra Biblical rabbinical literature that we hear some additional information which may give us a more reasonable interpretation.

NAS JUDE 1:7 *just as Sodom and Gomorrah and the cities around them, since they in the same way as these indulged in gross immorality and went after strange flesh, are exhibited as an example in undergoing the punishment of eternal fire.* NAS JUDE 1:8 *Yet in the same way these men, also by dreaming, defile the flesh, and reject authority, and revile angelic majesties.*

Rabbinical literature informs us that it was the giant Nimrod and his army who had come to Sodom and Gomorrah and ransacked them and their surrounding towns. And because Lot, Abraham's nephew was one of the families who lost everything to this marauding army, Abraham hunted him down and fought him and his army against overwhelming odds, and defeated them. Then, he returned all the booty to his nephew, and the cities and towns where he came from, including all of the women they had taken. Abraham had defeated a giant who led an army, just as David had defeated the terrifying giant Goliath and his army. Both did so trusting in God for their strength and courage.

Here's where we can put a different view on what happened. God returned all the wealth and women of these two cities and their surrounding towns through one of His people, Abraham. However, because of how terrifying the event had been, those towns were in fear and wanted more protection that they could count on, instead of relying on God who had rescued them. When they heard that there were two angels in town at Lot's house who were manifest in human form, the men of those towns had an opportunity and wanted to take it. After all, how often do you see angels manifest in human form?

They went to Lot's house because they saw the opportunity to somehow mix DNA with angels, with the intention of creating their own giant to defend themselves from any marauding armies who were led by a giant as what happened to them before. They did not decide to trust in the God of Abraham who had already rescued them, showing His power and willingness to protect them.

Instead, they opted to turn to the abominable pre-flood practice of creating giants through having union with angels. All the men of these two cities and towns agreed together on this course of action and then went to Lot's house to carry out the deed. What that looked like, and how it worked, one can only imagine, but obviously it involved sexual reproduction.

. . . just as Sodom and Gomorrah and the cities around them, since they in the same way as these indulged in gross immorality and went after strange flesh

Just before Jude says this in the above verse, he mentions the issue of the fallen angels who had union with natural women and created giants. In the above verse, he says Sodom and Gomorrah and their surrounding towns tried to indulge in the same activity—having reproduction with "strange flesh" –or celestial beings. God deemed this detestable practice reason enough to destroy the human race and the animal world. Now they were trying to do the same thing in these cities? God reinforced his judgment of how there was no tolerance for this by bringing swift judgment on these cities. It wasn't an issue of homosexuality and anal sex, but of crossbreeding the natural with the supernatural.

One might say that God had told Abraham that these cities had sinned and He was going to pour out judgment and destroy them. He decided this before the angels went there. So therefore, it wasn't about what they wanted to do to those two angels (according to that thinking), that brought about judgment.

Abraham had asked God to please see if He could search out righteous men and, therefore, save the towns his nephew lived in. Abraham did not realize the depths their evils had gone to. God sent His accompanying angels who were in human/natural form to honor Abraham. However, the towns proved to seek after the evil their hearts were bent on and intended to abuse these angels to carry out what they had already determined to do.

What this tells us is that these cities had together already decided to find a way to create their own giant, possibly even having had made some attempts already. They were engaging in the activities just as they did in the pre-flood times, and were determined to make that happen. That is why God was on His way to destroy them. So while the angels hesitated to carry out judgment per Abraham's request, the men of the city were ignorant of the impending doom for the decision they had made to pursue. As such, when the townspeople saw the angels in human form, much to their demise, they unanimously pounced on the opportunity to carry out their plan, and, in doing so, sealed their own fate.

Biblical rabbinical literature helps us affirm that 1) Nimrod was a giant, and 2) Nimrod and his army were the ones who ransacked these towns and whom Abraham rescued them from. Now, armed with that information—a few more key pieces of the puzzle—the same story makes totally different sense. Formerly, these additional facts were not available, leaving to the imagination an interpretation which skewed the story. Not only that, but the whole point was lost of why this story was included in the Bible. Jude's whole point and his words now make perfect sense with this context. Whereas before having this context, his words left a lot to be desired, according to the most common understandings derived from them.

Armed with this knowledge, we can have a richer understanding of why the second judgment of the flood came and how the continued pursuits of the same atrocities will contribute to bringing the third and final judgment of fire.

NIV Mt 24:36 "No one knows about that day or hour, not even the angels in heaven, nor the Son, but only the Father.

NIV Mt 24:37 As it was in the days of Noah, so it will be at the coming of the Son of Man.

NIV Mt 24:38 For in the days before the flood, people were eating and drinking, marrying and giving in marriage, up to the day Noah entered the ark;

NIV Mt 24:39 and they knew nothing about what would happen until the flood came and took them all away. That is how it will be at the coming of the Son of Man.

Notes

[2] Chinese. (2014). Retrieved September 2015, from Bible Probe: www.bibleprobe.com/chinese.htm

CHAPTER 5

Nimrod's Rebellion

(The other "savior")

Amp Ge 10:6 The sons of Ham: Cush, Egypt [Mizraim], Put, and Canaan.

Amp Ge 10:7 The sons of Cush: Seba, Havilah, Sabtah, Raamah, and Sabteca; and the sons of Raamah: Sheba and Dedan.

Amp Ge 10:8 Cush became the father of Nimrod; he was the first to be a mighty man on the earth.

NLT Ge 10:9 He was a mighty hunter in the Lord's sight. His name became proverbial, and people would speak of someone as being "like Nimrod, a mighty hunter in the Lord's sight."

Amp Ge 10:10 *The beginning of his kingdom was Babel, Erech, Accad, and Calneh, in the land of Shinar [in Babylonia].*

Amp Ge 10:11 *Out of the land he [Nimrod] went forth into Assyria and built Nineveh, Rehoboth-Ir, Calah,*

Amp Ge 10:12 *And Resen, which is between Nineveh and Calah; all these [suburbs combined to form] the great city.*

Nimrod (Gilgamesh) King of Ur founder of Babylon in the land of Shinar, the great city.

In Hebrew writings, they did not desire to immortalize evil men. So instead of giving their real name, they gave them a name that has the meaning of his way or sin. In Persian records, Nimrod's name is referred to as Gilgamesh. The writer of the book of Genesis called him Nimrod. The meaning of the name Nimrod is: "the one who made all of the people rebel against God" or "the rebel." Also incorporated into the meaning of that name is, "a mighty hunter before the Lord."

"He was a mighty hunter in the Lord's sight." Many translations say, "before the Lord." This doesn't reflect something good, rather something bad. "Before the Lord," or "in the Lord's sight," means in the Lord's face. In other words, in stark defiance of God. Not only was he a hunter of animals, but a hunter of men, whom he captured and enslaved to build these great cities.

Below is an excerpt from a Jewish historian describing Nimrod and his rebellion. Flavius Josephus of the Antiquities of the Jews — Book I. Josephus is a contemporary of Jesus.

Concerning the Tower of Babylon, and the confusion of Tongues.

1. Now the sons of Noah were three, Shem and Japhet, and Ham, born one hundred years before the deluge. These first of all descended from

the mountains into the plains, and fixed their habitation there; and persuaded others, who were greatly afraid of the lower grounds on account of the flood, and so were very loth to come down from the higher places, to venture to follow their examples. Now the plain, in which they first dwelt, was called Shinar. God also commanded them to send colonies abroad, for the through peopling of the earth; that they might not raise seditions among themselves, but might cultivate a great part of the earth, and enjoy its fruits after a plentiful manner. But they were so ill instructed, that they did not obey God. For which reason they fell into calamities, and were made sensible by experience of what sin they had been guilty of. For when they flourished with a numerous youth, God admonished them again to send out colonies. But they imagining the prosperity they enjoyed was not derived from the favour of God, but supposing that their own power was the proper cause of the plentiful condition they were in, did not obey him. Nay they added to this their disobedience to the divine will, the suspicion that they were therefore ordered to send out separate colonies, that, being divided asunder, they might the more easily be oppressed.

2. Now it was Nimrod who excited them to such an affront and contempt of God. He was the grand-son of Ham, the son of Noah: a bold man, and of great strength of hand. He persuaded them not to ascribe it to God, as if it was through his means that they were happy; but to believe that it was their own courage which procured that happiness. He also gradually changed the government into tyranny; seeing no other way of turning men from the fear of God, but to bring them into a constant dependence on his own power. He also said, "He would be revenged on God, if he should have a mind to drown the world again: for that he would build a Tower too high for the waters to be able to reach; and that he would avenge himself on God for destroying their fore-fathers."

3. [About An. 2520] Now the multitude were very ready to follow the determination of Nimrod, and to esteem it a piece of cowardice to submit to God: and they built a Tower; neither sparing any pains, nor being in any degree negligent about the work. And, by reason of the multitude of hands employed in it, it grew very high, sooner than any one could expect. But the thickness of it was so great, and it was so strongly built, that thereby its great height seemed, upon the view, to be less than it really was. It was built of burnt brick, cemented together with morter, made of bitumen; that it might not be liable to admit water. When God saw that they acted so madly, he did not resolve to destroy them utterly; since they were not grown wiser by the

destruction of the former sinners: but he caused a tumult among them, by producing in them diverse languages; and causing, that through the multitude of those languages, they should not be able to understand one another. The place wherein they built the Tower is now called Babylon: because of the confusion of that language which they readily understood before: for the Hebrews mean by the word Babel, Confusion. The Sibyll also makes mention of this tower, and of the confusion of the language when she says thus: "When all men were of one language, some of them built an high tower, as if they would thereby ascend up to heaven. But the Gods sent storms of wind, and overthrew the tower, and gave every one his peculiar language. And for this reason it was that the city was called Babylon." But as to the plan of Shinar, in the country of Babylonia, Hestiæus mentions it, when he says thus, "Such of the Priests as were saved took the sacred vessels of Jupiter Enyalius, and came to Shinar of Babylonia."[3]

Now we see by the Scriptures concerning Nimrod (above) that he was born in the second generation of those after the flood.

". . . he was the first to be a mighty man on the earth (Gen 10:8)". The reference to "mighty man" means a mighty warrior. The Bible tells us that he was the first to be a mighty warrior. He was the first to make war and conquer. It's important to take note that the Bible says he was the first.

Made King

. . . when Nimrod was eighteen years old, war broke out between the Hamites, his kinsmen, and the Japhethites. The latter were at first victorious, but Nimrod, at the head of a small army of Cushites, attacked and defeated them, after which he was made king over all the people on earth, appointing Terah his minister. It was then, elated by so much glory, that Nimrod changed his behavior toward Yhwh and became the most flagrant idolater[4].

"He was a mighty hunter in the Lord's sight" or before the Lord (Gen 10:9). We already discussed that Nimrod flagrantly and openly defied God. Since he became a warrior bent on conquest, it also includes being a hunter of men to oppress and enslave for his building projects.

".. . His name became proverbial, and people would speak of someone as being 'like Nimrod, a mighty hunter in the Lord's sight' (Gen 10:9)." This is telling us that Nimrod is the father of tyrants in all that he did. So much so, that in future generations if one was a type of tyrant, they would label that person as a "Nimrod." Here is an interesting note from Wikipedia below:

> In 15th-century English, "Nimrod" had come to mean tyrant.
>
> In 20th-century American English, the term is now commonly used to mean a dimwitted or a stupid person, a usage first recorded in 1932 and popularized by the cartoon character Bugs Bunny, who sarcastically refers to the hunter Elmer Fudd as "nimrod" as an ironic connection between "mighty hunter" and "poor little Nimrod", i.e. Fudd.[5]

Amp Ge 10:10 *The beginning of his kingdom was Babel, Erech, Accad, and Calneh, in the land of Shinar [in Babylonia].*

The beginning of his kingdom was Babel (Shinar), which became known as Babylon. We learned from the Jewish historian, Josephus, that it was God's command that man spread out across the whole earth, cultivate it, and live in peace. Nimrod was already in sin when he disobeyed this command and organized the people to gather together in the land (to be known as Babylon) in the plains of the Mesopotamian River Valley known at that time as Shinar.

He gathered people together for the expressed purpose of being strong, organized, and united, such as a king or a general of an army would desire. However, they had this fear that because of their sin and disobedience to God, He might bring another flood as He did before, especially since they were in the valley and had come down from the mountaintops to settle. Nimrod's solution was to build a tower so high it reached into the heavens. He was taking on the role of savior of the people of the earth in defense of the harsh judgments of God (Yahweh).

There were other purposes for the tower as Josephus tells us. The tower was a place where they practiced their idolatry and worshiped false gods. In addition, it was built so Nimrod could climb up to the heavens and kill Yahweh, thereby extracting vengeance against God for having killed His ancestors with the flood. In addition, as his self-proclaimed role of savior, he wanted to procure the safety of his people, all of the people of the earth. That is, so that they could practice the religion of Cain, which is to do as they willed and pleased, and Nimrod would thereby eliminate the threat of Yahweh punishing them by judging them with a death sentence for doing so. As a result, he pledged to the people that he would protect them from Yahweh and kill Him so that they could do as they pleased.

This did not please God that His people would defy Him, do as they pleased, and then take measures to war and defend themselves against Him. As a result, the Lord decided to first destroy the tower of Babel. Secondly, to spread them around the globe, dividing them up so they could not rally together, as was His command from the beginning to cultivate the whole earth (according to Josephus).

To ensure that this was the case, Yahweh took the people from speaking one common language to assigning 70 different languages for the 70 different nations of territories He assigned to the grandchildren of Noah. It was after God had done this that the tower they had built was referred to as the tower of Babel. It is because "babel" means confusion. Because of the tower, God had confused their languages so that they could not unite together for the reasons they had chosen, which was rebellion against Him. As such, the land that the tower was built on, Shinar, became known as Babylon, the kingdom of Nimrod.

Amp Ge 10:11 *Out of the land he [Nimrod] went forth into Assyria and built Nineveh, Rehoboth-Ir, Calah,*

Amp Ge 10:12 *And Resen, which is between Nineveh and Calah; all these [suburbs combined to form] the great city.*

However, the destruction of the tower of Babel, the spreading out of man around the globe, and the confusion of multiple languages did not sway Nimrod. Instead, he busied himself with pulling his kingdom back together and expanding it throughout Assyria, building many important cities there, some of which continue to exist today. Thus, he also became known in the Bible as "the Assyrian." It could be noted in the Bible that the center of Babylon or the city of Babylon eventually was called, "the great city." Accordingly, when you read in the Bible, and it refers to the great city, it is referring to Babylon and its center, or capital. Israel and Jerusalem, on the other hand, are referred to as, "The Beautiful Land."

Below are a few bullet points that are recorded about Nimrod which give a clarity about who he was in history and what his motives were. It also shows how all the different sources of documents across every culture in the area agree and hold Nimrod in the same light as the Bible.

- Nimrod surrounded his cities with high walls, and laid out its orchards and fields.
- He accomplished his building projects with forced labor, and his exhausted subjects groaned under his oppression.
- He was the first king on the earth.
- He was the first to wear a crown.
- He was the first to make war.
- He instituted the worship of Baal, false gods, and idols (feasting and reveling in sex orgies with temple priestesses, giving sacrifices to Baal).
- He started the practice of astrology.
- As a hunter, he was the first meat eater, and taught men how to eat meat.

- He was godlike in body and mind; he began his kingship as a cruel despot (a ruler with absolute power and authority; a person who exercises power tyrannically).
- He lorded over his subjects, raping any woman who struck his fancy, whether she was the wife of one of his warriors or the daughter of a nobleman. He had an insatiable lust for sex.
- "Tell the people not to worry about YHWH anymore, he is dead. I killed him over in the Lebanon mountains. So just live however you like, I will be your king and take care of you."
- He used great violence to force people to rely on him alone, instead of God.
- He wanted to rule the world.
- He forced people to worship false gods.
- He himself was lawless but lorded over the people his law.
- He was obsessed with finding a way to become immortal.
- He was also given the name Amraphel, which means "he whose words are dark." He was a vile blasphemer of Yahweh.
- He was said to have ruled for 400 years by 1 account, and died of a head wound.

"Now the multitude were very ready to follow the determination of Nimrod, and to esteem it a piece of cowardice to submit to God . . ." As noted, Nimrod was the great blasphemer of Yahweh. His determination was to live independent from God and to let the people of the earth do their own will. It was out of his "determination" that the following notions we live by today were born.

- It is the survival of the fittest
- God helps those who help themselves
- It' s dog-eat-dog
- God is nothing but a crutch for the weak
- Life is what you make out of it
- There is no such thing as destiny

- The world is your oyster
- Live hard and die young
- Life is too short
- You only live once
- Do as you will
- If you don't take care of yourself, then nobody else will (and so on . . .)

As Gilgamesh, in the ancient writings of Babylon, Nimrod says in regard to his quest to kill Yahweh, "If I fall, I will establish a name for myself. Gilgamesh is fallen, they will say, in combat with terrible Yahweh. But if I win, ... they will say, Gilgamesh, the mighty vanquisher of Yahweh!"

In another record this was recorded: After these adventures, Nimrod continued to reign wickedly. Four hundred years later, an angel in the form of a man appeared to him and exhorted him to repent, but Nimrod declared that he himself was sole ruler and challenged God to fight with him. Nimrod asked for a delay of three days, during which he gathered a considerable army . . .

Nimrod was the first king of the world; he was the self-proclaimed savior of the entire world. He saw Yahweh, the one true God, as a threat to mankind. He desired to bring back all of the pre-flood ways so that he could empower himself with every type of magic and evil that existed before the flood, having caused it. At 11 feet tall, he was considered a giant and was believed to be 2/3 god and 1/3 man.

In other words, Nimrod was a demigod, or as the Hebrews would say, a giant (Nephilim)—a product of being a hybrid of a fallen angel and a human. There is no other figure in the Bible or in recorded history that fits the role of antichrist, also known as the Assyrian, the beast, the lawless one, the desolator, and the abomination that causes desolation. In fact, by being called "the Assyrian," the Bible is telling us that Nimrod is the antichrist. But why call him the Assyrian? One of Nimrod's first acts of aggression was to conquer Assyria and be declared king of the world. In addition, he built cities in Assyria just as he had done in Babylon. Since this was his first conquest and he made Assyria great, it is only fitting that they would call him, "the Assyrian," because he was its founder. The most compelling evidence of this is the prophecy by Micah 5:1-15.

Birth of the King in Bethlehem

NAS MIC 5:1 *" Now muster yourselves in troops, daughter of troops; They have laid siege against us; With a rod they will smite the judge of Israel on the cheek.*

NAS MIC 5:2 *" But as for you, Bethlehem Ephrathah, Too little to be among the clans of Judah, From you One will go forth for Me to be ruler in Israel. His goings forth are from long ago, From the days of eternity."*

NAS MIC 5:3 *Therefore He will give them up until the time When she who is in labor has borne a child. Then the remainder of His brethren Will return to the sons of Israel.*

NAS MIC 5:4 *And He will arise and shepherd His flock In the strength of the LORD, In the majesty of the name of the LORD His God. And they will remain, Because at that time He will be great To the ends of the earth.*

NAS MIC 5:5 *This One will be our peace. When the Assyrian invades our land, When he tramples on our citadels, Then we will raise against him Seven shepherds and eight leaders of men.*

NAS MIC 5:6 *They will shepherd the land of Assyria with the sword, The land of Nimrod at its entrances; And He will deliver us from the Assyrian When he attacks our land And when he tramples our territory.*

NAS MIC 5:7 *Then the remnant of Jacob Will be among many peoples Like dew from the LORD, Like showers on vegetation Which do not wait for man Or delay for the sons of men.*

NAS MIC 5:8 *The remnant of Jacob Will be among the nations, Among many peoples Like a lion among the beasts of the forest, Like a young lion among flocks of sheep, Which, if he passes through, Tramples down and tears, And there is none to rescue.*

NAS MIC 5:9 *Your hand will be lifted up against your adversaries, And all your enemies will be cut off.*

NAS MIC 5:10 *"It will be in that day," declares the LORD, " That I will cut off your horses from among you And destroy your chariots.*

NAS MIC 5:11 *"I will also cut off the cities of your land And tear down all your fortifications.*

NAS MIC 5:12 *"I will cut off sorceries from your hand, And you will have fortune-tellers no more.*

NAS MIC 5:13 *" I will cut off your carved images And your sacred pillars from among you, So that you will no longer bow down To the work of your hands.*

NAS MIC 5:14 *"I will root out your Asherim from among you And destroy your cities.*

NAS MIC 5:15 *"And I will execute vengeance in anger and wrath On the nations which have not obeyed."*

Let's look at these verses a little closer:

Birth of the King in Bethlehem

NAS MIC 5:1 *" Now muster yourselves in troops, daughter of troops; They have laid siege against us; With a rod they will smite the judge of Israel on the cheek.*

NAS MIC 5:2 *" But as for you, Bethlehem Ephrathah, Too little to be among the clans of Judah, From you One will go forth for Me to be ruler in Israel. His goings forth are from long ago, From the days of eternity."*

Note: This is talking about the promised Messiah who will come out of Bethlehem (Jesus), "His goings forth are from long ago, From the days of eternity." This prophecy is pitting Jesus the Messiah against "the Assyrian" from the land of Nimrod. We are shown in these verses that this ultimate showdown in history will be the Christ vs. the antichrist. This tells us that the antichrist is the Assyrian.

NAS MIC 5:3 *Therefore He will give them up until the time When she who is in labor has borne a child. Then the remainder of His brethren Will return to the sons of Israel.*

Note: When it says, therefore He will give them up until the time . . .
This is speaking of how God will give His people over to Babylon, a.k.a.
the Assyrian, until Jesus returns (which can only happen after He is born)
bringing with Him those He has made His bride—celestial humans.

NIV Isa 14:24 *The LORD Almighty has sworn, "Surely, as I have planned, so it will be,
and as I have purposed, so it will stand.*

NIV Isa 14:25 *I will crush the Assyrian in my land; on my mountains I will trample
him down.*

By this, God had decreed that the final destruction of Nimrod, the
Assyrian and antichrist, will take place in Jerusalem. It will be after
Nimrod takes over Jerusalem and makes it the great city, the city of
Babylon, his headquarters. This will happen from the time of the great
tribulation until Jesus defeats him at the battle of Armageddon.

NAS MIC 5:4 *And He will arise and shepherd His flock In the strength of the LORD,
In the majesty of the name of the LORD His God. And they will remain, Because
at that time He will be great To the ends of the earth.*

Note: Verse 5:4 is talking about the 1,000 year reign of Christ after the
battle of Armageddon, when Jesus imposes His Kingdom over the whole
earth.

NAS MIC 5:5 *This One will be our peace. When the Assyrian invades our land, When
he tramples on our citadels, Then we will raise against him Seven shepherds and
eight leaders of men.*

NAS MIC 5:6 *They will shepherd the land of Assyria with the sword, The land of
Nimrod at its entrances; And He will deliver us from the Assyrian When he
attacks our land And when he tramples our territory.*

Note: Verse 6 is identifying Nimrod as the Assyrian.

When it says, "Then we will raise against him Seven shepherds and eight leaders of men," He is identifying the Assyrian/Nimrod as the beast. This is affirmed in Revelation:

NIV Rev 17:8 The beast, which you saw, once was, now is not, and will come up out of the Abyss and go to his destruction. The inhabitants of the earth whose names have not been written in the book of life from the creation of the world will be astonished when they see the beast, because he once was, now is not, and yet will come.

NIV Rev 17:9 "This calls for a mind with wisdom. The seven heads are seven hills on which the woman sits.

NIV Rev 17:10 They are also seven kings. Five have fallen, one is, the other has not yet come; but when he does come, he must remain for a little while.

NIV Rev 17:11 The beast who once was, and now is not, is an eighth king. He belongs to the seven and is going to his destruction.

"When the Assyrian invades our land . . ." (Micah 5:5). This prophecy is talking about the legacy of the antichrist. In this case and at that time, the Assyrian army, the largest army ever raised in the history of the world up to that time, invades and destroys all of Israel except for Jerusalem. This all happened during the contemporary time of Joel (who prophesied about it, and whose prophecy reflected the end times) as well as, the contemporary time when the Assyrian army invaded Israel.

However, during this occasion in history, the Assyrians destroyed all of Israel but were deterred by God before they could take over the city of Jerusalem. What that means is, in regards to crushing the Assyrian/the beast, he is talking about doing it not during those contemporary times but at the end times. It will be at the battle of Armageddon when Jerusalem will no longer be considered the holy city, but the great city, Babylon. When the antichrist rules the entire globe from Jerusalem, it is then that Jesus will defeat him, Babylon, and its spirit of defiance in totality.

God said in the prophecy that He will crush the Assyrian in His land, however, when the Assyrian army invaded Israel, it was not the time destined for that to happen. Likewise, the Assyrian (Nimrod) was dead and in the grave, neither had the Messiah been born yet. As a result, God restrained Assyria when they reached Jerusalem. They had laid siege to the city, starving it out, but failed to take it. It wasn't the right time yet. The right time to crush the Assyrian will be after the great tribulation when the headquarters of Babylon will be in Jerusalem, and Nimrod/the beast will have come to life in the holy temple.

NIV Isa 14:25 *I will crush the Assyrian in my land; on my mountains I will trample him down.*

Next, "Then we will rise against him Seven shepherds and eight leaders of men." Some mistakenly understand this to mean that we (meaning Israel) will rise against him (the antichrist/Babylon) seven shepherds and an eighth leader, shepherd meaning king.

It is not saying that Israel will raise up eight kings who will come against the antichrist and his Babylon/Assyria. We know this because these eight kings, we are told in verse 6, will shepherd the land of Assyria/the land of Nimrod, with a sword. What the prophecy is saying is that it is God's plan to raise up eight kings who will come into power over Babylon, the kingdom of Nimrod, which will punish and impede Babylon from becoming a global influence until the right time.

For example, the greatness of Assyria is taken over by Babylon through Nebuchadnezzar. In fact, Nebuchadnezzar and his army were one of the only armies who escaped the destruction of the Assyrian army as they laid siege on Jerusalem. Nebuchadnezzar and his Babylonian army were actually a part of that great army of Assyria until it was destroyed while laying siege to Jerusalem. Babylon then became great and attained its zenith under Nebuchadnezzar. Then, a king from Persia, king Cyrus invaded Babylon and took it over. After that, a king from Greece, Alexander the Great, destroyed Persia, which is Babylon, and he took it over.

Let us look at what Revelation says about these eight kings:

^{NAS REV 17:9} " *Here is the mind which has wisdom. The seven heads are seven mountains on which the woman sits,*
^{NAS REV 17:10} *and they are seven kings; five have fallen, one is, the other has not yet come; and when he comes, he must remain a little while.*

Note: "The woman" who sits . . . Is referring to the *Church Corrupt*, the Roman Church which has bound itself with the Roman Empire (jointly becoming the Holy Roman Empire). "The seven heads are seven mountains . . ." What this is saying is that the Assyrian/antichrist, who is the beast with seven heads, is, (during the time that John received this prophecy), the Roman Empire. Rome is the city which sits on seven hills.

It goes on to tell us that the beast with seven heads which is embodied by the Roman Empire also is the seven kings whose kingdoms are the kingdom of Babylon as founded by the first king, the Assyrian/Nimrod. These seven kings are the seven shepherds that Micah's prophecy was referring to.

It goes on to tell us that of the seven kings, five have come to pass, meaning their reign as Babylon's king have come and gone. The sixth one "is." What this means is that the empirical seat of the Roman Empire, when John was alive and received this prophecy, is the sixth king. All of the emperors of the Roman Empire, as long as it remained the Roman Empire, constitute the sixth king. We can understand it this way because Julius Caesar was the king who created the Roman Empire and even though he died, the Roman Empire continued as his legacy with his succession of kings.

Of the seventh king it says, "The other has not yet come; and when he comes, he must remain a little while." The seventh king is Pope Leo III who, after the Roman Empire was destroyed, raised it up again in 800AD, making the Church the ultimate authority of the empire. This new empire was known as the Holy Roman Empire. Just as the legacy of the Roman Empire (originated by Julius Caesar, and all its succeeding emperors until it was destroyed) can be called the sixth king, the succeeding popes, beginning with Leo III, combined are the seventh king.

However, in every case, the individual king that is named one of the seven is always the first king of that empire. The succeeding kings are merely the empirical legacy of the first king who created them. It is only after that kingdom is defeated (even if it is many years after the first king's death) that it has passed to the next of the seven kings/shepherds of Babylon with their ensuing empire.

It is the same for the first king of Babylon: Nimrod, the beast, and the antichrist. All these kingdoms which followed are his empirical legacy. Therefore, every one of them are referred to as Babylon. That's why it was said in the prophecy that the beast, Nimrod, had seven heads. All seven of these kings and empires were his or his empirical legacy. That is whether it is Babylon, Persia, Greece, Rome, or the Catholic Church. Their source and power came from what Nimrod established in Babylon and Assyria.

In Nebuchadnezzar's dream was a statue made up of four different metals and a fifth section of clay. Along the same lines, these four different metals which comprise one statue of a man are the four great empires of history; Babylon; Persia; Greece; and Rome. The fifth, whose material was not metal, but clay, is the woman who rides the beast, the *Church Corrupt*, who became the Holy Roman Empire.

We see by the statue that although it was a statue of one single man, it was comprised of five succeeding empires. This is in line with the view of seeing all of the succeeding emperors as one king/one empire, and all of the succeeding popes as the seventh king of the fifth empire of the statue (the clay). To see these five empires as one whole person, one would have to identify the person to be the one who founded Babylon, and was its first king. The other five empires are nothing more than the succeeding legacy of the first king by whose hand Babylon was created. This statue is the beast and the first king of the seven kings who founded Babylon, Nimrod. He is also known as "the Assyrian" because his kingdom began and was established by his first conquest, the nation of Assyria.

NAS REV 17:11 *"The beast which was and is not, is himself also an eighth and is one of the seven, and he goes to destruction.*

Note: Again, the beast is Nimrod whose legacy is all of the empires of Babylon combined, making up the kingdom of the beast. We are told in verse 11 that he "was," meaning he lived in the past. He "is not," meaning he is not alive at the time of this prophecy. And he is "to come", meaning as it says in Scripture: NAS REV 17:8 *" The beast that you saw was, and is not, and is about to come up out of the abyss and go to destruction.* This is saying that he will rise from the dead on his way to his destruction. That destruction is the lake of fire, where he will be thrown in, alive, along with his false prophet, after the battle of Armageddon.

It is verified that Nimrod was the first king of Babylon and will be the last because it says that the beast (Nimrod) himself is an eighth king, but he was also at one time one of the seven kings. He is the first king—whose entire legacy constitutes the balance of the kings and their empires, who also constitute the beast in its entirety with all its heads—as well as, the statue in its entirety. The beast will appear again when he comes up out of the grave and rules once more for forty-two months (3-1/2 years) as the antichrist. This is before being thrown alive into the lake of fire and after God's wrath has been poured out upon the earth (the kingdom of the antichrist), resulting in the battle of Armageddon.

NAS REV 17:12 *"The ten horns which you saw are ten kings who have not yet received a kingdom, but they receive authority as kings with the beast for one hour.*
NAS REV 17:13 *"These have one purpose, and they give their power and authority to the beast.*

Note: These ten kings are the rulers of the entire earth under the authority of the antichrist.

NAS REV 17:14 *"These will wage war against the Lamb, and the Lamb will overcome them, because He is Lord of lords and King of kings, and those who are with Him are the called and chosen and faithful."*

Note: Verse 14 is talking about the final showdown, the battle of Armageddon. This is when the beast and all that he is, including every trace of his legacy, will finally have that showdown he, Nimrod, has been waiting for. And of course, the verse ends with the result of that battle. Finally, the prophecy of Micah regarding the Assyrian and the great Assyrian army will have its end in this battle, and all prophecy will have been fulfilled. It is the same for Joel.

Let's get back to the prophesy of Micah, which tells us about the eight kings who will shepherd Babylon:

NAS MIC 5:7 *Then the remnant of Jacob Will be among many peoples Like dew from the LORD, Like showers on vegetation Which do not wait for man Or delay for the sons of men.*
NAS MIC 5:8 *The remnant of Jacob Will be among the nations, Among many peoples Like a lion among the beasts of the forest, Like a young lion among*

flocks of sheep, Which, if he passes through, Tramples down and tears, And there is none to rescue.

NAS MIC 5:9 *Your hand will be lifted up against your adversaries, And all your enemies will be cut off.*

Note: Verses 7-9 is talking about the Millennium Reign at which time all of the nations will serve Israel.

NAS MIC 5:10 *"It will be in that day," declares the LORD, " That I will cut off your horses from among you And destroy your chariots.*

NAS MIC 5:11 *"I will also cut off the cities of your land And tear down all your fortifications.*

NAS MIC 5:12 *"I will cut off sorceries from your hand, And you will have fortune-tellers no more.*

NAS MIC 5:13 *" I will cut off your carved images And your sacred pillars from among you, So that you will no longer bow down To the work of your hands.*

NAS MIC 5:14 *"I will root out your Asherim from among you And destroy your cities.*

NAS MIC 5:15 *"And I will execute vengeance in anger and wrath On the nations which have not obeyed."*

Note: In verses 10-15 the Lord is speaking to Babylon from its beginning to its end. He is declaring His intentions and His judgment. This is the end of the rebellion of Nimrod, the other savior, who would save all of the people of the world from the judgment of Yahweh so they might live under Nimrod's protection and do as they please.

Here is some more compelling evidence that it is Nimrod who is the beast and the antichrist. 2,000 years before John recorded the book of Revelation, Nimrod was recorded as having the following vision:

> It was he (Nimrod) *who saw in the sky a piece of black cloth and a crown; he called Sasan the weaver to his presence, and commanded him to make him a crown like it; and he set jewels in it and wore it. He was the first king who*

wore a crown. For this reason people who knew nothing about it, said that a crown came down to him from heaven.[6]

In John's prophetic vision some 2,000 years later in the book of Revelation he wrote:

NIV Rev 6:12 I watched as he opened the sixth seal. There was a great earthquake. The sun turned black like sackcloth made of goat hair, the whole moon turned blood red,

NIV Rev 6:13 and the stars in the sky fell to earth, as late figs drop from a fig tree when shaken by a strong wind.

Note: The sixth seal of verses 12 and 13 is referring to the beginning of the great tribulation. It is kicked off with an earthquake, and then it says the sun will turn black like a sackcloth made of goat hair. This represents the evacuation of the two witnesses, the Holy Spirit from the earth, and with Him, the *Church Pure* who are in union with Christ and possess within them the Spirit. The ensuing great tribulation is the time Jesus was talking about when He said:

NIV Jn 9:4 As long as it is day, we must do the work of him who sent me. Night is coming, when no one can work.

NIV Jn 9:5 While I am in the world, I am the light of the world."

And again, to the *Church Corrupt* who is found not in union with Christ and finds out they do not have the Spirit within them and their one talent which they buried is taken from them:

NIV Rev 3:15 I know your deeds, that you are neither cold nor hot. I wish you were either one or the other!

NIV Rev 3:16 So, because you are lukewarm—neither hot nor cold—I am about to spit you out of my mouth.

In verse 13, the stars who fell from the sky like late figs from a fig tree by a strong wind are the martyred Christians who were left behind and killed by the antichrist. The black sackcloth which blots out the sun is the spiritual darkness that Jesus warned about, a darkness which is a void of the presence of the Holy Spirit in the earth—a global desolation. It kicks off the 42 months of rule by the antichrist known as the great tribulation. Nimrod's vision showed him receiving a crown to rule the whole earth; with it comes a black cloth which represents a time of spiritual darkness. This parallels what John prophesied in Revelation:

NIV Rev 6:12 I watched as he opened the sixth seal. There was a great earthquake. The sun turned black like sackcloth made of goat hair.

Next, is Rev. 6:2:

NIV Rev 6:2 I looked, and there before me was a white horse! Its rider held a bow, and he was given a crown, and he rode out as a conqueror bent on conquest.
NIV Rev 6:3 When the Lamb opened the second seal, I heard the second living creature say, "Come!"
NIV Rev 6:4 Then another horse came out, a fiery red one. Its rider was given power to take peace from the earth and to make men slay each other. To him was given a large sword.
NIV Rev 6:5 When the Lamb opened the third seal, I heard the third living creature say, "Come!" I looked, and there before me was a black horse! Its rider was holding a pair of scales in his hand.
NIV Rev 6:6 Then I heard what sounded like a voice among the four living creatures, saying, "A quart of wheat for a day's wages, and three quarts of barley for a day's wages, and do not damage the oil and the wine!"
NIV Rev 6:7 When the Lamb opened the fourth seal, I heard the voice of the fourth living creature say, "Come!"
NIV Rev 6:8 I looked, and there before me was a pale horse! Its rider was named Death, and Hades was following close behind him. They were given power over a

fourth of the earth to kill by sword, famine and plague, and by the wild beasts of the earth.

Note: These four horsemen represent the beginning of the third judgment, which is the judgment of fire that God decided to bring upon the world. They were released simultaneously, when the whole world made Nimrod their king. The first horse, whose rider was bent on conquest and was granted a crown and a power to make war. He could, subsequently, draw power from the other 3 horsemen to take peace from the earth, enslave it, and have the authority to kill many of its people through the four winds of God's destruction. These four winds are, (1) the sword, (2) famine and starvation, (3) plagues of disease and natural calamities, (4) death by the animals of the earth (who, consequently, had not turned on man until after this judgment). In fact, all of these curses did not plague mankind in the post-flood world until the rebellion of Nimrod.

The crown was a judgment against the world which He granted to Nimrod, so that he could conquer and rule the entire world. Why would God judge the world a third time, so close to the time of the flood? The judgment of the flood, the second judgment, was brought upon the earth by the sin of Cain who demanded that God accept him for who he wanted to be, not who God willed him to be. As such, Cain and his legacy did whatever they desired, which brought on so much chaos and evil that it took the total destruction of the earth to destroy it.

Now here comes Nimrod, who is bent on reviving the ways of Cain during the pre-flood world. And not only that, he openly defies God and is willing to fight to the death to protect the people of the world from God so that they all may do as they will in rebellion to God, just as Cain did. It is after Nimrod shows his defiance by conquering Assyria through war that the people of the earth admire him so much for his defiance against Yahweh, that they made him king over all of them on the earth.

All of the people of the earth turned on their Creator and made Nimrod king over them to protect them from the consequences of doing as they willed in rebellion of God's will.

It is at this point that the Lord released the judgment of fire, which began by giving authority and power, through the four horsemen, to the Devil, who, in turn, gave it to his antichrist—Nimrod, the Assyrian. And it ends with the lake of fire. The entire natural universe will be cast into it for all of eternity, along with all who rebel against God from the beginning of the world to its end.

Many will say that the four horsemen are to be released at the end when the wrath of God is poured out. This is a faulty notion. The first four of the seals of judgment and redemption released in the earth happened at the time of rebellion by Nimrod and the people of the world, who idolized him for his defiance against Yahweh.

First, God tried to deter them by destroying the tower, spreading them around the world and confusing their language. However, Nimrod would not be deterred, but instead picked up the pieces and continued to build his empire. When all the people agreed and put themselves under him, famines began to come upon the earth, disease, natural disasters, and the animal kingdom turned on man, becoming a source of death for them. Likewise, it is then that Nimrod received his power by God to war, conquer, rule, and enslave the people.

Scripture tells us that when the power of the four horsemen, along with the antichrist, is utterly broken by Christ, once again the animals in the earth will be friends with man and no longer kill—the lion will lay with the lamb, and the child will play with the cobra. Likewise, disease and premature death will be a rarity, if not nonexistent, at that time.

Below are a few Scriptures that verify that the power of the four horsemen has already been released as a part of the judgment of fire which will plague the earth, allowing Nimrod the power to become the beast.

NIV 2Th 2:7 *For the secret power of lawlessness is already at work; but the one who now holds it back will continue to do so till he is taken out of the way.*
NIV 2Th 2:8 *And then the lawless one will be revealed, whom the Lord Jesus will overthrow with the breath of his mouth and destroy by the splendor of his coming.*

Note: When it refers to the one who holds back the power of the lawless one (Nimrod/the antichrist) and will continue to do so until he is taken out of the way, it is referring to the Holy Spirit. Right now and from the beginning, the power of the antichrist (the four horsemen) has been restrained and has not been allowed to have a global, unrestrained expression, but a limited expression. One of these measures of restraint we have already addressed, and that is the seven kings who shepherd Babylon. Instead of Babylon growing to global domination, it was stifled and set back when each ensuing empire defeated the previous in order to take over.

However, verse 8 tells us that it is when the Holy Spirit is taken from the earth (at the time of the rapture) that the antichrist will be revealed. At this point, he will begin his reign of terror, with no power restraining him. Days before that, however, he already appeared by coming alive from the grave and killing the two witnesses. He will finally have total global domination without the interference of God. This happens at the rapture when the absence of the Spirit of God (the desolation) begins. Years later, after His return to the earth, Jesus will destroy the antichrist at the battle of Armageddon,.

^{NIV Zec 6:7} *When the powerful horses went out, they were straining to go throughout the earth.*

Note: This Scripture in Zachariah uses the past tense saying the horses "went" out, meaning they had already been released. In addition, when it says they were straining to go throughout the earth, this agrees with the Scripture in 2 Thessalonians above. They were given a power to rule the whole earth, however, that power was restrained by the Holy Spirit and limited until the time of the end. In other words, although they were given power by God to do as they would, they were still, nevertheless, on a leash until the right time.

^{NIV Jer 24:10} *I will send the sword, famine and plague against them until they are destroyed from the land I gave to them and their fathers.'*

^{NIV Jer 42:17} *So will it be with all the men who set their faces to go to Egypt to dwell there temporarily; they will die by the sword, by famine, and by pestilence; none of them will remain or survive the evil that I will bring upon them.*

^{NIV Eze 14:21} *"For this is what the Sovereign LORD says: How much worse will it be when I send against Jerusalem my four dreadful judgments —sword and famine and wild beasts and plague—to kill its men and their animals!*

^{NIV Eze 6:11} *"Thus says the Lord GOD, 'Clap your hand, stamp your foot and say, "Alas, because of all the evil abominations of the house of Israel, which will fall by sword, famine and plague!*

The next set of verses (below) will be used to show how Nimrod is the beast and the antichrist:

The Beast out of the Sea

NIV Rev 13:1 . . . *And I saw a beast coming out of the sea. He had ten horns and seven heads, with ten crowns on his horns, and on each head a blasphemous name.*

Note: The beast coming out of the sea . . . Indeed, the waters represent the people of the earth—the sea of humanity, however, the waters also represent the waters of the flood. It says right before 13:1:

NIV Rev 12:15 *Then from his mouth the serpent spewed water like a river, to overtake the woman and sweep her away with the torrent.*

NIV Rev 12:16 *But the earth helped the woman by opening its mouth and swallowing the river that the dragon had spewed out of his mouth.*

NIV Rev 12:17 *Then the dragon was enraged at the woman and went off to make war against the rest of her offspring —those who obey God's commandments and hold to the testimony of Jesus.*

NIV Rev 13:1 *And the dragon stood on the shore of the sea.*

NIV Rev 13:1 . . . *And I saw a beast coming out of the sea. He had ten horns and seven heads, with ten crowns on his horns, and on each head a blasphemous name.*

Note: We see by these verses that although God had judged the earth with a flood, and it was Him who released and gave power for this judgment, it was the Devil who carried it out. The woman is the bride, or people of God throughout all of history of which there were only eight at this time. But the offspring of those on the ark who would obey God and not follow the Devil or his antichrist, this is who the Devil wanted to make war on.

Verse 16, which says the earth helped by opening its mouth and swallowing up the river (waters), is a representation of the mountains being heaved up to the extreme heights they are today, causing the ocean basins to be formed and allowing for dry land. The expression of "the earth . . . opening up its mouth," was used once before in the book of Genesis, when God was speaking to Cain and explaining to him that the earth had absorbed the blood of his brother, Abel—" the ground, which opened its mouth to receive your brother's blood . . . (Gen 4:11)."

Enraged that all humans were not killed, especially the ones who obeyed God, the Devil waited on the shore for the ark to come to dry land so he could make war on them and their offspring that would obey God.

Then John saw a beast coming out of the sea. The beast, the antichrist, who is the seed of Ham and comes out of the floodwaters, is the one the Devil is waiting to empower and to use to make his war on the people who obey God. It is Ham's seed, Nimrod, (Ham's grandson) who is the beast with seven heads, and will carry out the bidding of the Devil by making war on the people of God—the bride—throughout post-flood history.

Even before the eight disembarked the ark, the demise of the human race was present as a seed, carried by one who was on the ark. After disgracing himself to his father, Ham became the father of all who were evil in the earth and made themselves the enemies of God. Included are Nimrod and his people, Egypt and his nation, and Canaan and his nations (whose land God took away and gave to Abraham's descendents).

NIV Rev 13:2 The beast I saw resembled a leopard, but had feet like those of a bear and a mouth like that of a lion. The dragon gave the beast his power and his throne and great authority.

Note: This is making reference to the empires which are the legacy of the beast. The body resembled a leopard because the leopard is the empire of Greece (Alexander the Great). The entire western world has adopted the ways and thinking of the Greek culture; thus, the entire body is like a leopard. "A mouth like that of a lion . . ." This represents the Babylonian Empire under Nebuchadnezzar. In addition, the head having a mouth like a lion also represents the blasphemous mouth of the beast, Nimrod, who roars or rails against God. The feet like a bear represents the Persian Empire and the conquest of their armies wherever they had tread.

NIV Rev 13:3 One of the heads of the beast seemed to have had a fatal wound, but the fatal wound had been healed. The whole world was astonished and followed the beast.

Note: Verse 3 is speaking of the death and resurrection of Nimrod, the beast, and how the whole world will be amazed, following him as their savior to protect them against the judgment of God so they are free to do as they please. This will be in stark contrast to the cries of the two witnesses, who will warn the people to conform to God's will or be swept away by God's judgment. Only the beast will be able to shut up the two witnesses, showing himself (supposedly) able to protect the people of the world from the judgment of God. This same metaphor of the head wound also represents the fall of the Roman Empire in 476 AD. The healing of it was its restoration, which happened in 800 AD when Pope Leo III crowned Charlemagne, king of the Franks, emperor of the then Holy Roman Empire.

NIV Rev 13:4 Men worshiped the dragon because he had given authority to the beast, and they also worshiped the beast and asked, "Who is like the beast? Who can make war against him?"
NIV Rev 13:5 The beast was given a mouth to utter proud words and blasphemies and to exercise his authority for forty-two months.
NIV Rev 13:6 He opened his mouth to blaspheme God, and to slander his name and his dwelling place and those who live in heaven.
NIV Rev 13:7 He was given power to make war against the saints and to conquer them. And he was given authority over every tribe, people, language and nation.

NIV Rev 13:8 *All inhabitants of the earth will worship the beast—all whose names have not been written in the book of life belonging to the Lamb that was slain from the creation of the world.*

Scriptures that describe Nimrod's return from the dead:

NIV Isa 14:5 *The LORD has broken the rod of the wicked, the scepter of the rulers,*
NIV Isa 14:6 *which in anger struck down peoples with unceasing blows, and in fury subdued nations with relentless aggression.*
NIV Isa 14:7 *All the lands are at rest and at peace; they break into singing.*
NIV Isa 14:8 *Even the pine trees and the cedars of Lebanon exult over you and say, "Now that you have been laid low, no woodsman comes to cut us down."*

Note: This prophetic portion of Isaiah is referring to the time that the Lord has broken the power of Babylon, the Devil, his beast, and their power, the four horsemen. The time is after the battle of Armageddon.

NIV Isa 14:9 *The grave below is all astir to meet you at your coming; it rouses the spirits of the departed to greet you—all those who were leaders in the world; it makes them rise from their thrones—all those who were kings over the nations.*
NIV Isa 14:10 *They will all respond, they will say to you, "You also have become weak, as we are; you have become like us."*
NIV Isa 14:11 *All your pomp has been brought down to the grave, along with the noise of your harps; maggots are spread out beneath you and worms cover you.*

Note: The above verses are talking about the activity in Hades, the realm of the dead. Armageddon has just happened and the countless numbers that the antichrist/beast led into battle to oppose Jesus are all dead. All of the kings of the world over history are preparing themselves to meet the beast/Nimrod, because he has finally gone the way that they have—death. However, he does not. It says he will not join them in burial (Isa 14:20).

He will go to the lake of fire and not to Hades where they are. All of his proud and blasphemous words against Yahweh have proven to mean nothing, vain, having no substance or power behind them.

NIV Isa 14:12 *How you have fallen from heaven, O morning star, son of the dawn! You have been cast down to the earth, you who once laid low the nations!*

Note: Having fallen from heaven, O morning star, son of the dawn! Although they are speaking of the spirit and power behind Nimrod which is the Devil, they are really speaking to Nimrod himself. When the verses call him a morning star, they are talking about how he was the power that brought the dawning of a new age. In reality, it was an age of darkness and lasted only 3-1/2 years. Although he ruled the whole earth, it passed away, just as one day in the sun dawns and gives way to the night.

NIV Isa 14:13 *You said in your heart, "I will ascend to heaven; I will raise my throne above the stars of God; I will sit enthroned on the mount of assembly, on the utmost heights of the sacred mountain.*
NIV Isa 14:14 *I will ascend above the tops of the clouds; I will make myself like the Most High."*
NIV Isa 14:15 *But you are brought down to the grave, to the depths of the pit.*

Note: This is a reference to the Devil and the pride in his heart concerning his ambitions against God in heaven. However, and again, this is talking of the abomination that will happen in the temple. The image of the beast will be set up in the temple, the most holy and sacred place of God Almighty and of his Son, the Savior of the world. It is referring to what it says in Revelation: through the magic of the false prophet and through the image, Nimrod will be able to come up from out of the grave and the image will come alive, starting Nimrod's 3 1/2 years of rule.

However, the beast sees himself as the real savior of the world—the savior who saves the people of the world from having to conform to God, and from the judgment He plans to bring down on those who do not. He is taking this sacred place of the Savior of God and claiming it as his own (Jerusalem and the temple within), saying he is the true savior of the world. He (seemingly) proves it by showing that Yahweh cannot stop him from taking over this most holy and sacred place, and he sets himself up higher than those in the world that serve God (the stars in heaven), and likewise, even higher than the God they serve.

Yes, this is a story of two saviors. The first one, Jesus the Christ and Messiah who sacrifices His own life so that people may be born again with His disembodied Spirit, saved and forgiven of their sins. As a result, they will be reconciled and in obedience to the Father, avoiding the judgment of fire, which is about to come into completion over the whole earth and all of its inhabitants.

Then, there is the second savior who hates Yahweh, who despises His judgment of killing all of the people of the earth in a flood. Yahweh who will not let everyone do as they will, but will come up against them if they will not conform. He sees this as a great injustice, not understanding why he cannot do as he wills. In his hatred, he steps up to represent mankind and fight to the death against Yahweh to protect the people of the world from having to conform to Yahweh or suffer his judgments. In addition, he hates all those who would follow Yahweh and not follow him. If they do not follow him, there is only one choice: to denounce Yahweh and follow him, or be killed by him.

The majority of the people of the world would rather hate God as Cain did. They would rather do as they please and force God to accept them the way they are, and follow their other savior who would stop God from bringing His judgment. However, the last words of this verse show the vanity and futility of Nimrod's visions of grandeur:

NIV Isa 14:15 But you are brought down to the grave, to the depths of the pit.

The people are warned that the beast will not overcome.

NIV Isa 14:16 Those who see you stare at you, they ponder your fate: "Is this the man who shook the earth and made kingdoms tremble,
NIV Isa 14:17 the man who made the world a desert, who overthrew its cities and would not let his captives go home?"

Note: "The man" is the beast, Nimrod, who made the world believe they could fight and overcome God so they might do as they pleased. Just when he seemed superhuman, and invincible, he goes the way of everyone on the earth; he comes to the end of his life and all is lost in the battle of Armageddon, which the prophet is talking about right now. They can't believe this is the man who shook the world and could not be defeated in battle and who brought on the desolation and killed all of the saints during the great tribulation (the man who made the world a desert).

NIV Isa 14:18 All the kings of the nations lie in state, each in his own tomb.
NIV Isa 14:19 But you are cast out of your tomb like a rejected branch; you are covered with the slain, with those pierced by the sword, those who descend to the stones of the pit. Like a corpse trampled underfoot,
NIV Isa 14:20 you will not join them in burial, for you have destroyed your land and killed your people.

Note: You are cast out of the tomb like a rejected branch, is referring to Nimrod coming out of the Abyss, rising from the dead to carry out his havoc on the earth. As such, he is covered with the slain, the dead of countless numbers weigh upon him. This is talking about all of the people that he has killed from the beginning, climaxing with all the people he killed during the great tribulation and all who will die in the battle of Armageddon he seduced into fighting Jesus.

However, verse 20 says, "you will not join them in burial." It is talking about the aftermath of the battle of Armageddon. All who oppose Jesus in that battle will die that day. All of the dead, including the Devil himself, are confined to Hades, awaiting the last day of judgment. However, Nimrod—the beast—and his false prophet who came up out of the earth (the grave) had their time in Hades already. They departed from the grave as it says above; "cast out of your tomb." They had come back to life according to what God had granted them. They were raised from the dead before the last day and on their way to their destruction of being thrown alive into the lake of fire for their second death. In between Hades and their second death, they had been granted to do as God put in their hearts.

We are told in the Bible that everyone at the battle of Armageddon dies except for the false prophet and the beast, Nimrod. They are instead thrown alive into the lake of fire, even 1,000 years before the last day when all who are destined for it will finally join them.

NIV Isa 14:20 ... *The offspring of the wicked will never be mentioned again.*

NIV Isa 14:21 *Prepare a place to slaughter his sons for the sins of their forefathers; they are not to rise to inherit the land and cover the earth with their cities.*

Note: Verses 21-23 (above and below) speak specifically of the battle of Armageddon and how, on that day, all traces of Babylon and their leader, the beast, will be destroyed forever—cut off—with no remnant to ever rise again. This prophecy makes reference to what Nimrod's empire consists of—great urban centers or cities. These cities will be destroyed and they will not be allowed to rise again.

The word antichrist means, the other savior (christ) and also the antithesis of the Christ. In the days of Nimrod, and as a part of His judgment of fire, God granted that Nimrod could have the destiny he has been given because of his heart. By empowering Nimrod as the antichrist, God is able to expose in the hearts of the people of the world who they really wanted to serve.

However, the choice is not what you would think. The choice is this, serve God or serve self. It is this choice which determines the Savior/savior you line up under. If one chooses to serve God and conform to Him, Jesus becomes his Savior who reconciles him to God. On the other hand, if one chooses to serve self, and desires to do as he wills, then the antichrist will become his savior. This individual will rally with those under the other savior who will fight God to the death and oppose Him, so they may do as they will.

NIV Isa 14:22 "I will rise up against them," declares the LORD Almighty. "I will cut off from Babylon her name and survivors, her offspring and descendants, " declares the LORD.

NIV Isa 14:23 "I will turn her into a place for owls and into swampland; I will sweep her with the broom of destruction, " declares the LORD Almighty.

A Prophecy Against the Assyrian

NIV Isa 14:24 The LORD Almighty has sworn, "Surely, as I have planned, so it will be, and as I have purposed, so it will stand.

NIV Isa 14:25 I will crush the Assyrian in my land; on my mountains I will trample him down. His yoke will be taken from my people, and his burden removed from their shoulders. "

NIV Isa 14:26 This is the plan determined for the whole world; this is the hand stretched out over all nations.

Note: The Lord is saying that it is His plan to crush Nimrod, the beast, in Jerusalem. It is there in Israel that He has determined to destroy him, and break his power and oppression over the people of God. This plan of the Lord is a part of His judgment on the whole world. This will be a global struggle and a time in which every person must choose where he stands.

The next Scripture that speaks of Nimrod raising from the dead is in Daniel:

Amp Da 9:26 And after the sixty-two weeks [of years] shall the Anointed One be cut off or killed and shall have nothing [and no one] belonging to [and defending] Him.

Note: This is referring to the crucifixion of Christ, bringing 69 of the 70-7's to an end. There is only 1-7 left which will bring fulfillment of the 70-7's prophecy. That is 7 years. However, there is a gap between the end of the 69-7's (7-7's & 62-7's) when Jesus is crucified and the beginning of the 70th-7. That gap has lasted so far about 2,000 years and is called the Gospel Age or the Church Age. The Church Age is a time where there is a pause taken between the 69th-7 and the 70th-7. This pause is a direct result of the people of God (the Jews) rejecting Him and not becoming His bride. This pause created time for God to pick for Himself a bride from among the gentiles. However, when the 70-7's resume, all that is left is one 7 year period.

Amp Da 9:26b . . . And the people of the [other] prince who will come will destroy the city and the sanctuary. Its end shall come with a flood; and even to the end there shall be war, and desolations are decreed.

Note: "The people of the other prince," is referring to the Romans and their army, who are the people. They did indeed come in 70AD and destroyed the city and the temple. When it says, "the people of the [other] prince who will come . . ." the "who will come" does not go to the people that will destroy, meaning they ("the people") will come. It goes to the prince, meaning the other prince who will come. That prince is not referring to Jesus, nor is it referring to the 8th king—the antichrist. The prince in question is who Revelation refers to as the false prophet, or the beast out of the earth.

Amp Da 9:27 *And he shall enter into a strong and firm covenant with the many for one week [seven years]. And in the midst of the week he shall cause the sacrifice and offering to cease [for the remaining three and one-half years]; and upon the wing or pinnacle of abominations [shall come] one who makes desolate, until the full determined end is poured out on the desolator.*

Note: "And he shall . . ." "he" is referring to again the false prophet, who is the second beast who comes out of the earth (the grave). It is he who will make a covenant with many nations. It says that the covenant will last for one 7—seven years. That seven years is the final seven of the 70-7's. When he makes these treaties, it shall mark the beginning of the last seven years of the 70-7's. The treaties with many nations are a precursor to the sovereign rule that the antichrist will impose over the entire globe. These treaties with "many nations" may look more like a league of nations that submit to a joint authority, which the false prophet is in authority over. Much like NATO or the United Nations or even the League of Nations after WWI.

Note: Although it is common to think that this final seven years of the 70-7's is the time of the antichrist and of the great tribulation, it is not true. If you read what Daniel was told at face value, we will learn differently. At the beginning of this last seven years of the 70-7's, the antichrist has not yet come. He comes after it is over. The 70-7's that God decreed holds back the end times. They cannot come until the decree has run its course. Let us look carefully at what Daniel was told, and it will be clear to see that the antichrist/the beast does not come until the final seven years is complete.

Amp Da 9:27 *. . . And in the midst of the week* (of years/seven years) *he shall cause the sacrifice and offering to cease*

Daniel was told that at the midpoint of the last seven years of the 70-7's (3-1/2 years after the last seven began) the false prophet (the second beast) will impose some sort of authority that he has through this league of nations, banning the Jews from making sacrifices in the temple.

NAS DA 12:11 *"From the time that the regular sacrifice is abolished and the abomination of desolation is set up, there will be 1,290 days.*
NAS DA 12:12 *"How blessed is he who keeps waiting and attains to the 1,335 days!*

Furthermore, we learn from Daniel that after the midpoint (3-1/2 years from the start of the last seven), exactly 1,290 days later, the source of abomination is "set up." That puts the setup of the image 30 days after the end of the last seven. 3-1/2 years or 1,260 days to the midpoint after the treaties were made, adding another 3-1/2 years or 1,260 days brings the conclusion of the last 7. From there, 30 days later or 1,290 days after the midpoint, the image of the beast is setup in the temple by the false prophet. In other words, at the midpoint of the last seven when the sacrifices are abolished, there will be no activity in the temple until after the last seven is over. It is then, 30 days later, that the false prophet will begin worshiping the image of the beast in the temple, making it active once again.

The first question is: What is this abomination? We are told in Revelation that it is a image of the antichrist/beast/abomination/Nimrod, the Assyrian. It is the statue that Nebuchadnezzar saw in his dream. This is what is said about the false prophet who is the second beast:

NIV Rev 13:12 *He exercised all the authority of the first beast on his behalf, and made the earth and its inhabitants worship the first beast, whose fatal wound had been healed.*
NIV Rev 13:13 *And he performed great and miraculous signs, even causing fire to come down from heaven to earth in full view of men.*

NIV Rev 13:14 *Because of the signs he was given power to do on behalf of the first beast, he deceived the inhabitants of the earth. He ordered them to set up an image in honor of the beast who was wounded by the sword and yet lived.*

The next question is: Now that the final 7 has concluded, what happens next? To follow this timeline given to Daniel, 1,290 days after the sacrifices were ordered to cease the false prophet, the prince of the antichrist, sets up an image of the antichrist in the temple. 3-1/2 years after the midpoint brings the final 7 to its conclusion. 30 days later, he then begins his abominable forms of worshiping the antichrist/the beast in the temple, thereby deceiving the whole earth into worshiping the beast through the image in the temple. He does so by performing signs and wonders that are similar to what the two witnesses are executing.

Now enters the beast/antichrist, Nimrod (the vanquisher of Yahweh):

Amp Da 9:27 *and upon the wing or pinnacle of abominations [shall come] one who makes desolate*

Daniel is then told that at the pinnacle or at the climax or height of these abominable forms of worshiping the beast, the image will actually come alive and start killing all who will not worship him. It is at this point that Nimrod, the beast and antichrist, comes up out of the Abyss from death to rule the entire globe.

NIV Rev 13:15 *He was given power to give breath to the image of the first beast, so that it could speak and cause all who refused to worship the image to be killed.*

NIV Rev 17:8 *The beast, which you saw, once was, now is not, and will come up out of the Abyss and go to his destruction. The inhabitants of the earth whose names have not been written in the book of life from the creation of the world will be astonished when they see the beast, because he once was, now is not, and yet will come.*

Going backwards, we know from what Daniel was told that it is some amount of time within a 45 day time period, beginning after the false prophet sets up the image in the temple and his abominable magic builds up to a fever's pitch, that the antichrist comes up out of the grave and (somehow), through the image, becomes alive again. That 45 days is merely the difference between the 1,290 day mark after the sacrifices are ordered to cease (when the image is then built in the temple), subtracted from the 1,335th day after the sacrifices were ordered to cease of which Jesus said, "How blessed is he who keeps waiting and attains to the 1,335 days!"

What was going on that the whole world let this false prophet build an image which brings to life a person of the past who would save the people of the earth from God? Ever since half way through the last 7 years of the 70-7's, the false prophet has caused the sacrifices to cease. At the same time, the Lord answers this dastardly action by releasing the two witnesses during the last 3-1/2 years of the last seven.

NIV Rev 11:3 And I will give power to my two witnesses, and they will prophesy for 1,260 days, clothed in sackcloth."

NIV Rev 11:4 These are the two olive trees and the two lampstands that stand before the Lord of the earth.

NIV Rev 11:5 If anyone tries to harm them, fire comes from their mouths and devours their enemies. This is how anyone who wants to harm them must die.

NIV Rev 11:6 These men have power to shut up the sky so that it will not rain during the time they are prophesying; and they have power to turn the waters into blood and to strike the earth with every kind of plague as often as they want.

NIV Rev 11:7 Now when they have finished their testimony, the beast that comes up from the Abyss will attack them, and overpower and kill them.

NIV Rev 11:8 Their bodies will lie in the street of the great city, which is figuratively called Sodom and Egypt, where also their Lord was crucified.

NIV Rev 11:9 For three and a half days men from every people, tribe, language and nation will gaze on their bodies and refuse them burial.

NIV Rev 11:10 The inhabitants of the earth will gloat over them and will celebrate by sending each other gifts, because these two prophets had tormented those who live on the earth.

NIV Rev 11:11 But after the three and a half days a breath of life from God entered them, and they stood on their feet, and terror struck those who saw them.

NIV Rev 11:12 Then they heard a loud voice from heaven saying to them, "Come up here." And they went up to heaven in a cloud, while their enemies looked on.

What prompted the false prophet to construct the image of Nimrod? Ever since he caused the sacrifices to end, these two witnesses have been speaking to the whole world. They are a nuisance to the false prophet as well as to all the people of the earth who will not heed their message but go on living according to their own will and desires. Just as Moses was to Pharaoh and the people of Egypt. It says of the two witnesses:

NIV Rev 11:6 These men have power to shut up the sky so that it will not rain during the time they are prophesying; and they have power to turn the waters into blood and to strike the earth with every kind of plague as often as they want.

NIV Rev 11:10 The inhabitants of the earth will gloat over them and will celebrate by sending each other gifts, because these two prophets had tormented those who live on the earth.

In the last half of the last 7, the two witnesses are the Lord's answer to the forced end of sacrifices in the temple. It is also His last effort to appeal to the people of the earth before the end, which is decreed to be after the 70-7's conclude.

Perhaps all the international animal rights groups will be appalled at the killing of animals at the temple, thinking it a crude, archaic, and barbaric practice. The international protest and unrest caused by it will lead the false prophet, heading the league of nations, to impose upon Israel that they must cease for the cause of peace and international law.

The norm in the world will be groups such as these who speak out, saying that there is no difference between the murdering of animals as there is if you kill a man (even as they do now). This way of thinking no longer regarding a human life with reverence and as something more sacred than the animals of the earth, who have no soul. Special interest groups such as the gay community, same sex marriages, and the breakdown of gender identity, all together are bringing a global movement to undo the laws and designs of God. During that time, it will be as the bumper sticker calls for everyone to "coexist."

Like a shark who tastes blood and goes into a feeding frenzy, the spirit of antichrist will consume the world into fanaticism, radicalism, hostility and violence to gain what they think will be a utopian world in which everyone is given acceptance. There will be a global mantra calling for acceptance and coexist. Anyone who opposes this will be considered archaic and barbaric, and he will be treated with prejudice and hostility. Cain will finally have his way—acceptance without conformity.

NIV Ge 4:5 *but on Cain and his offering he did not look with favor. So Cain was very angry, and his face was downcast.*

NIV Ge 4:6 *Then the LORD said to Cain, "Why are you angry? Why is your face downcast?*

NIV Ge 4:7 *If you do what is right, will you not be accepted? But if you do not do what is right, sin is crouching at your door; it desires to have you, but you must master it."*

NIV Ge 4:8 *Now Cain said to his brother Abel, "Let's go out to the field." And while they were in the field, Cain attacked his brother Abel and killed him.*

However, the two witnesses will speak and prophesy against the trend the whole world will adopt. The whole world will hate them; even the Church will be against them. The two witnesses will seemingly be the only thing in the way of total humanism and acceptance. The people of the world will try to shut them up and stop them, with murder in their hearts. However, they won't be successful. The two witnesses will release fire, curses, droughts, and miraculous signs as Moses did, to try to wake people up from their madness. The people of the world will not see conformity as their solution but, instead seek protection from these men, so that they may do as they will and make the earth what they want.

Moses caused Aaron's staff to become a snake and Pharaoh's court magicians also made snakes, however, the snake of Moses swallowed up the snakes of Pharaoh's "magicians." The antichrist's false prophet will also call down fire to make the people believe his source of power is as powerful as that of the two witnesses.

It is important to note that just as in the case of Pharaoh's court magicians who deceived the people of Egypt and made them feel safe under Pharaoh's power, the signs and wonders of the false prophet, too, are vain and impotent wonders. The snakes from the staffs of Pharaoh's magicians were all swallowed up by the snake from Aaron's staff. The false prophet calling down fire is just a display, like a trick a magician can perform. However, these tricks will deceive the people into feeling safe under the authority of the beast, whom this false prophet performs for.

On the other hand, when the two witnesses execute miraculous wonders, it has nature changing power, in that it can stop the rain from falling, create global droughts, turn whole bodies of water into blood, create natural disasters, loose diseases and catastrophes, and finally call down fire that consumes and kills anyone who would try to stop them. Just as in the days of Pharaoh and Moses, the whole world will be deceived into thinking that the false prophet of the beast has a genuine power to resist God.

After 3-1/2 years, and at the end of the 70th-7, the false prophet will know exactly what to do, and the whole world will desire him to do it. They will want anything, at any cost, that will put an end to these two witnesses so that they might be free to have it all the way they want it—a world at peace ruled by acceptance—the way and religion of Cain. He will give them what they want, which is the other christ—the antichrist, the beast and vanquisher of Yahweh.

The false prophet will build an image of Nimrod, the vanquisher of Yahweh, and the whole world will see it as the solution to overcome their problem, the two witnesses, who no one can stop or kill. Then, sometime within 45 days after the image is set up, he will call the beast out of the grave (the Abyss), and the image will come alive.

Revelation says it was an "image" that the false prophet set up in the temple, which could also be interpreted as a statue. When we think of an image or a statue, we think of something made of stone or bronze. However, it is within the realm of reason to believe the image of the beast set up in the temple could be made of something else, like flesh, for example. Maybe as a result of human sacrifice. The false prophet, it says, is given the power to give the image breath. Jesus calls the image which comes alive and stands in the temple, "an abomination," a "beast," the one who makes desolate or "the desolator." He is a Frankenstein, a freak and an abortion of nature. Jesus admonishes us: when you see him come to life and he is standing in the Holy temple, don't even take time to go inside to get a coat! Run for your lives!

Like Sodom and Gomorrah who did not desire or trust the God of Abraham to protect them and keep them safe, but instead wanted a freak of nature, a giant, a half-supernatural half-natural being to protect them.

Just like the men of renown, or demigods of old before the flood, the world will want Nimrod to come back from the grave and protect them from the wrath of God and these two witnesses.

We will have come full circle, back to what facilitated the judgment of fire being released, along with the four horsemen. In those days, just a couple generations after the flood, the whole world made Nimrod king over them because of his defiance against God. Now the false prophet claims that the risen Nimrod will protect them from the wrath of Yahweh so that they may do as they please.

He does not let them down. The first order of business of the antichrist (Nimrod the vanquisher of Yahweh back from the dead) will be to leave the temple and kill the two witnesses, who have just finished testifying for 1,260 days. He kills the unkillable and satisfies the whole world. The two witnesses have been testifying since soon after the sacrifices in the temple were ordered to cease. Now they have been quieted by the antichrist.

NIV Rev 11:7 Now when they have finished their testimony, the beast that comes up from the Abyss will attack them, and overpower and kill them.

NIV Rev 11:8 Their bodies will lie in the street of the great city, which is figuratively called Sodom and Egypt, where also their Lord was crucified.

NIV Rev 11:9 For three and a half days men from every people, tribe, language and nation will gaze on their bodies and refuse them burial.

NIV Rev 11:10 The inhabitants of the earth will gloat over them and will celebrate by sending each other gifts, because these two prophets had tormented those who live on the earth.

NIV Rev 11:11 But after the three and a half days a breath of life from God entered them, and they stood on their feet, and terror struck those who saw them.

NIV Rev 11:12 Then they heard a loud voice from heaven saying to them, "Come up here." And they went up to heaven in a cloud, while their enemies looked on.

However, Jesus tells Daniel:

NAS DA 12:12 *"How blessed is he who keeps waiting and attains to the 1,335 days!*

The three blessings

1) *NAS DA 12:12* *"How blessed is he who keeps waiting and attains to the 1,335 days!*

2) *NAS REV 14:13* *And I heard a voice from heaven, saying, "Write, 'Blessed are the dead who die in the Lord from now on!' " "Yes," says the Spirit, "so that they may rest from their labors, for their deeds follow with them."*

3) *NAS REV 16:15* *"Behold, I am coming like a thief. Blessed is the one who stays awake and keeps his clothes, so that he will not walk about naked and men will not see his shame."*

Jesus makes a similar blessing on three occasions. The third occasion is concerning His return, the 1,000 year reign, and the ensuing battle of Armageddon right before He conquers the antichrist and then rules the world for 1,000 years.

NAS REV 16:15 *("Behold, I am coming like a thief. Blessed is the one who stays awake and keeps his clothes, so that he will not walk about naked and men will not see his shame.")*
NAS REV 16:16 *And they gathered them together to the place which in Hebrew is called Har-Magedon.*

When He says, "keeps his clothes, so that he will not walk about naked and men will not see his shame." He is not talking about being dressed with fabric. He is saying: blessed is he who is not deceived into fighting against Him at Armageddon and instead guards his life.

Our soul is clothed with our body. It will be a shameful thing to be killed, disembodied, and then confined to Hades at this point. After all the people have gone through surviving the great tribulation and the outpouring of God's wrath, all they have to do is wait a few more days (until after the battle of Armageddon), then Jesus will rule the earth. Then everything will be healed. They will go from torment to bliss if they can guard their life and trust the Lord for just a few more days, at that point. He is basically saying, "Hang in there and don't lose heart by turning on Me, because all who come out to fight My authority in order to take over the whole earth will die in that battle." Truly, those who guard their lives (their clothes) will be blessed if they make the right choice, in those last few days before Jesus takes over the earth.

The second occasion is the harvest of grapes, when the blood of the Church flows like a river 4 to 5 feet deep for over 200 miles. That river will be the blood spilled of the remainder of the saints who do not go up as wheat—the rapture (Rev 14:17). They were not found in union with Christ and must endure the great tribulation. They will be killed during the reign of Nimrod, the antichrist. However, Jesus says of them that they too will be "blessed."

NAS REV 14:12 *Here is the perseverance of the saints who keep the commandments of God and their faith in Jesus.*

NAS REV 14:13 *And I heard a voice from heaven, saying, "Write, 'Blessed are the dead who die in the Lord from now on!'" "Yes," says the Spirit, "so that they may rest from their labors, for their deeds follow with them."*

It is these that constitute the great multitude and become celestial humans (given clean white robes [celestial bodies not a robe of fabric]) during the first resurrection (Rev 20:5-6). This is the first resurrection of the dead that is exclusively for those who die during the great tribulation. Their death while hanging onto their profession will not be in vain. They will be the bride of Christ, celestial humans, and rule the earth with Him for 1,000 years. Yes, this group will be truly blessed.

The first occasion is in regard to the end of the 70-7's, when the beast comes out of the Abyss at the onset of the great tribulation. Jesus proclaims a blessing for those who can endure, while hanging onto their faith, and not be swayed by the pressures and attitudes of the rest of the world—to give acceptance without conformity, and hatred of the two witnesses and their message. This blessing, 1,335 days after the sacrifices were ordered to stop and 75 days after the end of the 70th-7, is a very similar blessing Jesus gives on the other two occasions. The third group Jesus gives a blessing to the people who patiently guard their lives and stay alive becoming a part of His millennium reign on the earth, by surviving the battle of Armageddon. The second group He blesses, who, by hanging onto their profession of faith, do not worship the beast or take his mark, even at the cost of their lives.

Exactly 1,335 days after the sacrifices in the temple are forced to end, and days after the beast comes out of the grave to have his time to destroy the two witnesses and the Church, the Spirit of Jesus will withdraw from the earth. He will bring up with Him the *Church Pure* and the two witnesses. That is, if we wait for Him without losing heart or falling in line with the attitudes and the pressures of the rest of the world; if we do so and attain all the way to the 1,335th day, we will be blessed. Without falling dead, we will become celestial humans, and we will not have to endure the hell on earth that follows our departure. It is the rapture, the harvest of wheat, when Jesus personally collects His bride (Rev 14:14).

On all three occasions Jesus gives a blessing to those who under pressure go against the sway of the entire world who defy God. They will be a small minority and they will have to honor God at a time when the whole world will be against them and their very lives will be on the line. It is no wonder that when Jesus gives a list of those who will not enter the

Kingdom, it is the cowards who are mentioned first and the unbelievers, second.

NIV Rev 21:6 *He said to me: "It is done. I am the Alpha and the Omega, the Beginning and the End. To him who is thirsty I will give to drink without cost from the spring of the water of life.*

NIV Rev 21:7 *He who overcomes will inherit all this, and I will be his God and he will be my son.*

NIV Rev 21:8 *But the cowardly, the unbelieving, the vile, the murderers, the sexually immoral, those who practice magic arts, the idolaters and all liars—their place will be in the fiery lake of burning sulfur. This is the second death."*

Jesus affirms these three blessings in the following Gospel verses, Mk 13:13, Mt 10:22, Mt 24:9-15.

NIV Mt 24:9 *"Then you will be handed over to be persecuted and put to death, and you will be hated by all nations because of me.*

NIV Mt 24:10 *At that time many will turn away from the faith and will betray and hate each other,*

NIV Mt 24:11 *and many false prophets will appear and deceive many people.*

NIV Mt 24:12 *Because of the increase of wickedness, the love of most will grow cold,*

NIV Mt 24:13 *but he who stands firm to the end will be saved.*

As a final note: We know that the great tribulation begins after the 70th-7 is finished, the image comes alive and starts by him killing the two witnesses. 1,335 days after the sacrifices were ordered to stop and within 45 days after the image is set up in the temple, Jesus will rapture His bride. We know this because Jesus told us:

Amp Mt 24:15 *So when you see the appalling sacrilege [the abomination that astonishes and makes desolate], spoken of by the prophet Daniel, standing in the Holy Place—let the reader take notice and ponder and consider and heed [this]. . .*

Who is the false prophet who calls the antichrist from among the dead? Where does he come from and who will he be?

The Beast out of the Earth

NIV Rev 13:11 *Then I saw another beast, coming out of the earth. He had two horns like a lamb, but he spoke like a dragon.*

Note: Many believe that because this second beast has two horns like a lamb and speaks like a dragon, he will be gentle at first and everyone will believe him and follow him as a result. Then he will turn into a tyrant just when everyone is hooked. They even accredit this characteristic to the antichrist. This is a total misinterpretation of this verse.

First of all, it is describing the second beast who also comes up from the grave (the earth). How do we know this is true that out of the earth means out of the grave or Hades? First off, there is no other sensible understanding of that saying. Secondly, when the battle of Armageddon is over and all are dead, there are only two standing—this second beast (the false prophet), and the antichrist who is the first beast (Nimrod). Unlike all who have died in this battle and are thrown, disembodied, into Hades, these two are thrown alive into the lake of fire to endure a second death.

All men die, becoming disembodied, and all will be raised from the dead by the Lord on the last day and once again have a body. This is for the purpose of all being judged on their own merit and then, as a result, either going on to eternity, or being thrown alive into the lake of fire, dying a second death for all of eternity. Hades is a temporary holding place until the last day. It is also to be done away with when it is emptied on the day of judgment. After it is emptied, it too is thrown into the lake of fire. The lake of fire is forever!

Both the antichrist and the false prophet are prematurely risen to life from out of Hades and given a body to face judgment with. Only, they have a deal; they are allowed to walk the earth for a short time before having their eternal fate. As it says, out of the Abyss on his way to his destruction (the lake of fire). Or as in Daniel . . . until the full determined end is poured out on him, the desolator (the lake of fire). Both of them have no right to go back to Hades. It is time for their second death, which is to be thrown alive into the lake of fire, as they have already received their resurrected body so they may face judgment.

NIV Rev 19:19 *Then I saw the beast and the kings of the earth and their armies gathered together to make war against the rider on the horse and his army.*
NIV Rev 19:20 *But the beast was captured, and with him the false prophet who had performed the miraculous signs on his behalf. With these signs he had deluded those who had received the mark of the beast and worshiped his image. The two of them were thrown alive into the fiery lake of burning sulfur.*
NIV Rev 19:21 *The rest of them were killed with the sword that came out of the mouth of the rider on the horse, and all the birds gorged themselves on their flesh.*

These two will inhabit the lake of fire all alone for 1,000 years. It says that even the Devil is captured and held in the Abyss, so that he may be loosed once again for the time of Gog-Magog at the very end of the 1,000 year reign of Christ. Only after this time will the Devil finally be thrown into the lake of fire.

It will not be for at least 1,000 years after the battle of Armageddon and finally after the last day—the day of judgment—that anyone else will finally enter the lake of fire. At that time, they will no longer be alone, because the whole natural universe (the earth, Hades, fallen angels), along with all who have been judged as goats, doomed to suffer a second death, will be thrown alive into the lake of fire for all of eternity. The lake of fire is the end of the judgment of fire that began with the Devil receiving the power of the four horsemen and giving authority to his antichrist.

In proof of the second beast being a person who came back to life after once dying: if the second beast did not come out from Hades after having lived once before, he would have been thrown into Hades where angels and the souls of disembodied men are being held for the last day. Unless he had died once already he would not have been sent to the lake of fire to face his second death as Revelation tells us.

In regards to the two horns like a lamb, it is better understood this way: a sheep that is in its first year of life is called a lamb. During the time between 1 year old and two, it is called a yearling. When it is full grown, it is called a ram for males and an ewe for females. A sheep is only a lamb for one year. So this could be interpreted as the second beast having power for only one cycle of time, or in this case a week of years which is seven years. In addition, in the Bible, horns represent power. And the lamb has short nubs for horns, not like those of a ram who has had time for his horns to develop.

The proper interpretation is that the second beast will have a short time of power and will be subordinate to the first beast.

NIV Rev 13:12 *He exercised all the authority of the first beast on his behalf, and made the earth and its inhabitants worship the first beast, whose fatal wound had been healed.*

Note: It has to be asked why this second beast is exercising all the authority of the first beast. And why is he rallying all the people of the earth to worship the first beast? And why is he the one that is pulling all the nations together under treaties to eventually consolidate the world under a one world government? Why isn't the first beast doing this? The answer we already learned in Daniel. The second beast is a kind of John the Baptist for the antichrist, or an anti-John-the-Baptist, if you will. He is paving the way and readying the earth for the first beast, Nimrod, the antichrist, or the "other savior."

NIV Rev 13:13 *And he performed great and miraculous signs, even causing fire to come down from heaven to earth in full view of men.*

NIV Rev 13:14 *Because of the signs he was given power to do on behalf of the first beast, he deceived the inhabitants of the earth.*

Note: The second beast will perform these miraculous signs for three and one half years before the antichrist comes. We also know from Revelation that the two witnesses will be killed after the end of the last 7 years of the 70-7's, as soon as the antichrist comes alive. We also know that they will witness for three and one half years previous to their death. They will call down fire on anyone who tries to kill them.

Who then is this second beast, or false prophet? This is how he is referred to in Daniel:

Amp Da 9:26 *. . . And the people of the [other] prince who will come will destroy the city and the sanctuary*

He is called the other prince who will come, prince over the people who will destroy Jerusalem in 70AD. In addition, in Daniel 9:27, we are told that the last 7 years of the 70-7's is ushered in with his short-lived 7 years of power. It is during his time of power that the last 7 occurs. Similarly, the exile to Babylon was decreed to happen during the 70 years of power given to Nebuchadnezzar and his Babylon. The 7-7's began during the time of power given to Darius and the Persian Empire. The end of the 62-7's was brought to a conclusion during the time of power given to Julius Caesar and the Roman Empire. Again, Daniel tells us that the last 7 is during the time of power given to the false prophet, the second beast out of the earth, the other prince who will come.

The first time we hear of him is in Daniel when he is called, the prince of the people who destroy Jerusalem. The second time we hear of him is in Revelation where he is called the second beast out of the earth. The third time he is identified as the false prophet who deceives the world on behalf of the first beast.

Let's put this all together. We know that Babylon, the kingdom of Nimrod the beast, was a kingdom that started soon after the flood. At that time, Babylon had been an empire which, over time, had as its legacy 5 ensuing empires. All of this combined together is the empire of the beast throughout history. We saw in the Scriptures that the Lord predestined 7 kings who conquered Babylon and resumed it by taking it over. The Lord did this as a way to slow down the process of Babylon reaching global supremacy, until the right time.

The people who came and destroyed Jerusalem were the Romans. The Roman Empire was the fourth empire in succession to the others Daniel was shown. The king of that empire was Julius Caesar and all the ensuing Caesars continued the Roman Empire. However, Babylon (being the Roman Empire represented as iron in the statue) was to give way to the 5th and final empire before it was to be turned back over to the beast upon his return to the living.

That 5th empire became what is known as the Holy Roman Empire, the feet of clay mixed with iron. The iron represents the powerful king of the Franks, Charlemagne, and the clay, the Roman Catholic Church. In 800AD, the Catholic Church became Babylon, known also in Scriptures as the whore of Babylon who rides the beast. The prince of that empirical legacy of Babylon is Pope Leo III and all the ensuing popes ever since.

Why the whore who rides the beast? After the Roman Empire was destroyed, the Church lost its power over the people. It was the Roman Empire who empowered the Church and enforced the power of the pope. When Leo III became pope, there were many factions of the Church against him. He was very much threatened, and in addition, had no power base. So he decided to revive the Roman Empire. Pope Leo III accomplished this by taking the powerful king of the Franks, Charlemagne, and declaring him king of what Pope Leo III gave birth to; the Holy Roman Empire. A revival and creation made by Pope Leo III. In doing so, he would strengthen his position as pope and once again have a very strong power base.

King Charlemagne jumped at the opportunity. It is recorded in history that on December 25th, Christmas day 800AD, he was ordained by the pope as the king of the Holy Roman Empire. As soon as the crown was placed upon his head by the pope, he realized he was outfoxed. He was outraged by the epiphany that by the pope being the one who put the crown on his head, naming him king of the Holy Roman Empire, the pope was above him as an authority and not below.

So indeed, Pope Leo III, representing the Catholic Church, prostituted her by empowering his office with secular force through the king of the Franks, making him the leader of the empire of the beast, Babylon. And with bit and bridle in the king's mouth, the whore of Babylon (the Catholic Church) imposed herself through the power of the beast. Together they made the Holy Roman Empire—the clay and iron mixed together. The power of Babylon is the whore's beast of burden.

In going further in the prophecy of the statue, the legs of the statue were made of iron (the Roman Empire). Then the feet gave way to a combination of iron mixed with clay (the Holy Roman Empire, consisting of the king of France and the pope of the Catholic Church). The final portion of the statue, the lower part of the feet, was the clay mixed with iron (the Catholic Church). The Catholic Church still exists today, and the prince of the Catholic Church is the office of pope and whoever holds it.

Yes, Babylon, even the Roman Empire, is alive today and spiritually empowered through the beast. It is alive and well as the Roman Catholic

Church. However, because it no longer has military might behind it, it is only fitting this current phase of Babylon is the one of clay mixed with iron.

The prince to come, spoken of in Daniel, who also is the beast that came out of the earth (the false prophet), will sign a treaty with many nations, kicking off the last 7 years of the 70-7's. He will build an image of Nimrod in the temple and will bring him back from among the dead to save the world from God and from the two witnesses.

It also says in Daniel in regard to this prince to come, that his people will destroy Jerusalem. History reveals that "his people" was the Roman Empire. This prince to come will be a pope of the Roman Catholic Church. He will be a pope who will be declared dead (even if only for an hour or so) but will miraculously come back to life.

Here is a picture of that time to come, the time of the beast:

The two witnesses come from heaven to the natural world to warn the world of the coming judgment. They will perform miraculous signs like causing droughts and calling down fire; they will rail against the *Church Corrupt,* speaking many condemning things against the Church. They will do this from Jerusalem. People will hate them, including all the mainstream denominational churches. They will be called doomsday prophets, and the Church all over the world will disown them as from the Devil because they will say such evil things about the Church. They will speak against the trend of the world and the Church, which is to give acceptance without conformity under the guise of bringing peace. The whole world will watch in disdain of them, and some will try to kill them because, like Moses, they will call down plague after plague, totally interrupting life as it is known on the earth.

The reason the *Church Corrupt* hates the two witnesses is because the Church has become the religion of Cain. It has done this by following the secular world, which has adopted and imposed the ways of Cain— acceptance without conformity to God's design.

While this is going on, there is a backdrop of the second beast/false prophet, who also speaks from Jerusalem. He, too, is considered a superhuman being who came up from out of the dead. He is shouting, "Peace, peace!" While the two witnesses are proclaiming the coming judgment, the false prophet is doing his thing. He unites many of the nations of the earth under treaties, predisposing the world for a one world government, therefore making it ready for Nimrod, the antichrist. He, too, is calling down fire to show that he is just as powerful as the two witnesses. He sells the whole earth on worshiping the first beast, calling him the real savior of the world who will protect them from the likes of the two evil witnesses (in the eyes of the world and the *Church Corrupt*).

The image he has built in the temple is the very statue Nebuchadnezzar saw in his dream. This image is of the founder of Babylon and of its empires, Nimrod. Somehow, the image comes to life, and Nimrod is embodied again from out of the Abyss. The first thing he does is kill the two witnesses, a feat no human could accomplish.

The beast, Nimrod, then goes on a rampage, killing anyone who believes in God. He declares that he is going to save the world from God and from His judgments. He will not tolerate another judgment from God, such as the flood that killed his ancestors. This is why Jesus said:

NAS MT 24:15 *"Therefore when you see the ABOMINATION OF DESOLATION which was spoken of through Daniel the prophet, standing in the holy place (let the reader understand),*
NAS MT 24:16 *then those who are in Judea must flee to the mountains.*

MT 24:17 " *Whoever is on the housetop must not go down to get the things out that are in his house.*

NAS MT 24:18 *9" Whoever is in the field must not turn back to get his cloak.*

NAS MT 24:19 *"But woe to those who are pregnant and to those who are nursing babies in those days!*

NAS MT 24:20 *"But pray that your flight will not be in the winter, or on a Sabbath.*

The two witnesses lay dead three and one half days with no one tending to their bodies. The whole world celebrates their death. They party and exchange gifts, because the (other) savior of the world has brought an end to them.

However, at the end of those three and one half days of laying dead in public, they rise to their feet and terrify the whole world. Some time afterwards, they are called up to heaven because their job is finished. But it does not stop there. There is a huge earthquake that destroys a tenth of the city of Jerusalem and kills seven thousand people. It does so because another phenomena takes place. The Spirit of God, who is restraining the power of the antichrist, withdraws from the earth, leaving it in the time of darkness Jesus warned us about, saying of it that no one can work. He said, "As long as I am in the world, I am the light of the world." By His Spirit, Jesus has been with us since the day of Pentecost. When He withdraws, there is no light in the world, and the work that the Father has given Him to do stops.

However, one thing remains. Jesus promised something when He said this:

NIV Jn 14:15 *"If you love me, you will obey what I command.*

NIV Jn 14:16 *And I will ask the Father, and he will give you another Counselor to be with you forever—*

NIV Jn 14:17 *the Spirit of truth. The world cannot accept him, because it neither sees him nor knows him. But you know him, for he lives with you and will be in you.*

NIV Jn 14:18 I will not leave you as orphans; I will come to you.

Note: Jesus promises to not leave us like orphans, and that the Holy Spirit will live in us forever!

NIV Jn 14:19 Before long, the world will not see me anymore, but you will see me. Because I live, you also will live.
NIV Jn 14:20 On that day you will realize that I am in my Father, and you are in me, and I am in you.

Note: The world will not see him anymore because He will withdraw His Spirit from the earth when the antichrist comes at the end of the last 7 years of the 70-7's. Jesus goes on to say that because He lives, we too will live. "On that day . . ." What day? The day He withdraws His Spirit from the world, and the world will not see Him anymore. He goes on to tell us that the day His Spirit leaves the world, leaving it in a global desolation, is the day that we will realize that He is in His Father and we are in Him, and He is in us.

How will Him withdrawing His Spirit from the earth cause us to realize that He is in us and us in Him and Him in the Father? Elementary! When He withdraws His Spirit from the earth and brings it back to where He is, all those who are found in union with Him, and His Spirit in them, will suddenly find themselves clothed in a celestial body, standing before the throne of the Father and that of the Son. In other words, He is saying that we don't have to believe Him now because we will know what He says is all true on that day when we suddenly find ourselves in heaven where He is, without having died.

Sadly, for the rest of the Christians, who are so by profession only, not living in union with Christ and not found controlled by His Spirit, Jesus will, at that time, take from them what little Spirit they have within them. What this means is that when He withdraws His Spirit from the earth, the Christians who are not controlled by His Spirit—the power of union that would make them one—is not strong enough in them to lift them up with the Holy Spirit. They will remain during the great tribulation, and the Holy Spirit that was in them will be taken away and retreat to heaven for 3-1/2 years, along with those who are in union with Him. They will live through a time of darkness in which God will not intervene, prayers will go utterly unanswered. They will have to believe and live without a sense of God present in their lives. This is what is known as a global desolation—a total absence of the presence of God in the earth.

As the parable of the one talent goes, those who metaphorically have buried their one talent because they are afraid they might not do it right when they act from the Spirit, will lose what little Spirit they do have. If there is any doubt that the parable of the talent is talking about the rapture and who is left behind during the great tribulation, then listen to how Jesus ends this parable:

NIV Mt 25:28 " *'Take the talent from him and give it to the one who has the ten talents. NIV Mt 25:29 For everyone who has will be given more, and he will have an abundance. Whoever does not have, even what he has will be taken from him. NIV Mt 25:30 And throw that worthless servant outside, into the darkness, where there will be weeping and gnashing of teeth.'*

What the master says of those who invested the talent was, "Come and share your master's happiness!" When he says, "Come," He means come to heaven and be raptured. When He says to the others, throw them into the darkness where there will be weeping and gnashing of teeth, He is referring to abandoning them to the time of darkness which is the great tribulation.

Since they were a Christian by profession, they will have to prove their profession true by holding fast to their testimony, not taking the mark of the beast, or worshiping the beast. They must do so even at the cost of their lives.

He will carry out on the rest of the Church what He had promised He would do to them: to vomit them out of His mouth, so they are no longer in Him and Him in them. He will leave them, the *Church Corrupt*, alone to endure the great tribulation "where there will be weeping and wailing and gnashing of teeth." He will close the door on the 5 virgins, " 'Sir! Sir!' they said. 'Open the door for us!' "But he replied, 'I tell you the truth, I don't know you.'." He will, in essence, be saying, since His Spirit was not in you and you were not in union with Him, He never knew you.

NIV Mt 7:21 *"Not everyone who says to me, 'Lord, Lord,' will enter the kingdom of heaven, but only he who does the will of my Father who is in heaven.*
NIV Mt 7:22 *Many will say to me on that day, 'Lord, Lord, did we not prophesy in your name, and in your name drive out demons and perform many miracles?'*
NIV Mt 7:23 *Then I will tell them plainly, 'I never knew you. Away from me, you evildoers . . .'*

However, they have a hope! If they endure the great tribulation or even are put to death during it, but they hold fast to their testimony and do not worship the beast or take his mark, they will be raised from the dead. They will be given white robes (celestial bodies) while taking their place as His bride and a part of the great multitude. They will take part in the first resurrection, and not have to wait until the last day to be judged worthy to go on to eternity, nor will they face the second death. The first resurrection is for them alone.

NIV Rev 20:1 *And I saw an angel coming down out of heaven, having the key to the Abyss and holding in his hand a great chain.*
NIV Rev 20:2 *He seized the dragon, that ancient serpent, who is the devil, or Satan, and bound him for a thousand years.*

NIV Rev 20:3 He threw him into the Abyss, and locked and sealed it over him, to keep him from deceiving the nations anymore until the thousand years were ended. After that, he must be set free for a short time.

NIV Rev 20:4 I saw thrones on which were seated those who had been given authority to judge. And I saw the souls of those who had been beheaded because of their testimony for Jesus and because of the word of God. They had not worshiped the beast or his image and had not received his mark on their foreheads or their hands. They came to life and reigned with Christ a thousand years.

NIV Rev 20:5 (The rest of the dead did not come to life until the thousand years were ended.) This is the first resurrection.

NIV Rev 20:6 Blessed and holy are those who have part in the first resurrection. The second death has no power over them, but they will be priests of God and of Christ and will reign with him for a thousand years.

You may say, who will pick the other savior and stand against the true God desiring to be saved from Him and His judgments?

The answer is, the whole world. Look what is going on right now in the world. Even look at the one example we brought up in talking about the religion of Cain, which was homosexuality. If you agree with the Bible and see homosexuality as a sin, then you are condemned by society and called archaic and a homophobic, even one who fosters violence.

A Miss America winner was attacked, brought to ruin, and lost her title simply because she stated that according to her Christian faith, homosexuality is a sin and is not natural.

In a university in Florida, a man was suspended because he refused his professor's demand to write on a paper taped to the ground the name "Jesus" and then stomp on it.

The federal court system has made a ruling allowing for gay marriages. Pastors in Kentucky who have had prison ministries for most of their lives are being forced to sign a paper stating they will never again characterize homosexuality as a sin. If they do not sign, as some have not, they lose their ministry, and their status as a Christian pastor is revoked with the state.

While this book is being written, there is a Christian county clerk in Kentucky who refuses to allow her name to be on the certificates of marriages of same sex people, and will not sign them. She has been put in jail for not doing so. Likewise, one state after another are allowing cross-dresser and transgender people the right to choose which public restroom to use, male or female. It is being made a legal right to choose your own gender, even to reject being identified as one gender or the other.

One after another, Christian pastors, as well as whole denominations, are giving acceptance without conformity in the name of unity and brotherhood to gays, their marriages, and to whatever belief systems that are out there.

It is not the Gospel of Christ to attack and force God's Church and believers to accept what God calls sin. This is the "other gospel" from the "other savior" who promises to save the people of the world from Yahweh's wrath, and who will, under his protection, let them do as they will, and be accepted.

Whole contingencies of groups are rising up and condemning the ways of God in the Bible and those who believe in it. They are lovers of themselves. They, like Cain and Nimrod after him, would force God to accept them how they desire to be. They twist around the meanings of God's word so they can make it mean whatever they will. Yes, they do not want a Savior who will give them a Spirit that causes them to obey God, but they want a savior who will make God accept them for what they want to be. Look around, the whole world is ripe for the other savior who will give them acceptance to do as they please. By force, the real way of salvation is being stifled, discredited, and made false.

The people of the world will hold so fast to the other savior who will come up against the true God, that even when God's wrath is poured out, making the earth virtually unlivable, they will not repent of any of their ways. They will, instead, raise their fists to heaven and curse God for bringing down on them His judgment, because He won't let them live the way they will. They will fiercely serve self and, out of hatred, refuse to serve God. They will believe that the right thing to do is to join the antichrist savior in a last stand showdown at the battle of Armageddon, accepting death over conformity to God. This is how resolute they are in wanting a savior who will save them from the God who would have them conform to His will.

Things will not get better, but worse. A tide is turning. The whole world is rising up to force the religion of Cain and the gospel of Nimrod on the Christian Church, making them believe that it is the way of Jesus to give acceptance without conformity. This movement will consider the world at peace when their ways are achieved because everyone can do as they will, without being condemned or criticized. The choice is clear, serve God or serve self. You will not be able to stand in the middle any longer. The Lord has seen to it.

The importance of the gospel of the antichrist, which is acceptance without conformity (enforcement of the way of Cain by the antichrist), cannot be underestimated. It is, in fact, the whole ball of wax and the problem with man. The way of Cain brought on the judgment of water, which flooded the whole earth and killed all but a few people. The rebellious defiance of Nimrod, who would fight God to the death to protect the world from God's judgment so that people could follow the way of Cain, brought the judgment of fire. Before it is finished being carried out, this judgment of fire will destroy the entire universe and all who live in it

From within, there is a pressure on the Church of God to adhere to the gospel of the antichrist and give acceptance without conformity (as is the example with homosexuality). From the outside, even the laws of this nation supposedly founded on Christian principles exert a pressure on the Church, even with legal and criminal consequences, trying to force the Church to adapt to the gospel of the antichrist—to give acceptance without conformity to God's will. Things are as described in the passage of Ezekiel:

NIV Eze 8:17 He said to me, "Have you seen this, son of man? Is it a trivial matter for the house of Judah to do the detestable things they are doing here?

The world sees it as a small compromise that will unite all men and cause them to be on equal ground. The *Church Pure* cannot and will not compromise in the area of conforming to God and His will. It is this rub that will divide the Church in such a way that there will be nothing short of a civil war within it! Unfortunately, the side who has a true New Covenant relationship with Christ will be relatively small in number compared to the corrupt side of the Church. This rub of acceptance without conformity, the gospel of the antichrist, will provoke the nations and all of society to severely persecute and take away the rights of the Christians who follow the Gospel of Christ. They will eventually genocide them.

Knowing this helps us understand how after God pours out His wrath on the earth as judgment, the people, it says, will raise their eyes to heaven and shake their fists, cursing God. They will refuse to love a God who would judge and kill people for simply doing what they will. Especially when they have a savior who will help them do as they will.

NIV Rev 9:20 *The rest of mankind that were not killed by these plagues still did not repent of the work of their hands; they did not stop worshiping demons, and idols of gold, silver, bronze, stone and wood—idols that cannot see or hear or walk.*
NIV Rev 9:21 *Nor did they repent of their murders, their magic arts, their sexual immorality or their thefts.*

NIV Rev 16:8 *The fourth angel poured out his bowl on the sun, and the sun was given power to scorch people with fire.*
NIV Rev 16:9 *They were seared by the intense heat and they cursed the name of God, who had control over these plagues, but they refused to repent and glorify him.*
NIV Rev 16:10 *The fifth angel poured out his bowl on the throne of the beast, and his kingdom was plunged into darkness. Men gnawed their tongues in agony*
NIV Rev 16:11 *and cursed the God of heaven because of their pains and their sores, but they refused to repent of what they had done.*

The Church is under a great deception. This statement is not the rantings of a couple of doom and gloom prophets. The Bible tells us that this is the case, especially in the end times. We may say that we are celebrating Christ, the true Savior of the world, in celebrating Christmas, however, here are some facts: December 25th is not the birthday of Christ, the true Savior of the world; He was not even born at that time of the year. It is the birthday of Nimrod, the other savior, or the antichrist. 2,000 years before Jesus was born, they celebrated Nimrod as the savior of the world on December 25th. Furthermore, they pray for him to rise from the dead. They did so with Christmas trees decorated with ornaments, and lights. They had 12 days of celebration, going door-to-door singing, exchanging gifts, partying, and worshiping the sun god, Nimrod. The concept and focus on the manger scene for Christmas has its roots with Nimrod—his wife and their child. The worship of Ishtar (better known as Samiramis who [supposedly] gave a virgin birth of Tammuz) is the root of the cult practice of the worshiping of Mary, the mother of Jesus. Easter is not even a Jewish or Christian word. It is the name of Nimrod's wife Ishtar (Semiramis). She started the cult practice of praying for Nimrod to rise from the dead and save the people of the world.

> Tradition shows that all the observances from other cultures and peoples throughout ancient times were mere copies or modifications of the original story of Nimrod, his wife Semiramis and their son Tammuz. The story is told that the wife of Nimrod, the King of Babylon, after the death of her husband, claimed she had been supernaturally impregnated by the Sun god and gave birth to Tammuz. When Tammuz was forty years old, he went hunting and was killed by a wild boar. His mother and her family mourned for 40 days, at the end of which Tammuz was brought back from the dead. So, Lent is evidently the time when Tammuz is remembered and mourned during the "Fast of Tammuz." The Wycliffe Bible Commentary states, "Mourning for the god was followed by a celebration of resurrection." [7]

She claimed that Tammuz (her son) was the reincarnate Nimrod, and that he (Tammuz) would rise from the dead again to rule the world.

Part of their ritual in the Spring was to fast, mourn, and weep for Tammuz to rise from the dead and come back to life. They did this for 40 days (which has found its practice in the Church as the 40 days of fasting for Lent). In addition, they would worship the sun at sunrise as a part of this festival, which has spilled over into the Church with its traditional sunrise service for Easter. As a part of worshiping Ishtar's fertility, eggs were worshipped to represent fertility. Rabbits were also worshiped because they are known to multiply exceedingly.

One might say that it's tradition, and for the children. However, during the celebration of Nimrod on the last five days of December, children were sacrificed as a way to appease the sun god so that he would grant one more year. Another might say, "But I'm worshiping Jesus, not Nimrod or Ishtar on Christmas and Easter." In answer, the Lord said to Ezekiel about this very practice, "is it a trivial matter . . . ?" He assured Ezekiel, indeed it was not.

Idolatry in the Temple

NIV Eze 8:1 *In the sixth year, in the sixth month on the fifth day, while I was sitting in my house and the elders of Judah were sitting before me, the hand of the Sovereign LORD came upon me there.*

NIV Eze 8:2 *I looked, and I saw a figure like that of a man. From what appeared to be his waist down he was like fire, and from there up his appearance was as bright as glowing metal.*

NIV Eze 8:3 *He stretched out what looked like a hand and took me by the hair of my head. The Spirit lifted me up between earth and heaven and in visions of God he took me to Jerusalem, to the entrance to the north gate of the inner court, where the idol that provokes to jealousy stood.*

NIV Eze 8:4 *And there before me was the glory of the God of Israel, as in the vision I had seen in the plain.*

NIV Eze 8:5 *Then he said to me, "Son of man, look toward the north." So I looked, and in the entrance north of the gate of the altar I saw this idol of jealousy.*

NIV Eze 8:6 *And he said to me, "Son of man, do you see what they are doing—the utterly detestable things the house of Israel is doing here, things that will drive me far from my sanctuary? But you will see things that are even more detestable."*

NIV Eze 8:7 *Then he brought me to the entrance to the court. I looked, and I saw a hole in the wall.*

NIV Eze 8:8 *He said to me, "Son of man, now dig into the wall." So I dug into the wall and saw a doorway there.*

NIV Eze 8:9 *And he said to me, "Go in and see the wicked and detestable things they are doing here."*

NIV Eze 8:10 *So I went in and looked, and I saw portrayed all over the walls all kinds of crawling things and detestable animals and all the idols of the house of Israel.*

NIV Eze 8:11 *In front of them stood seventy elders of the house of Israel, and Jaazaniah son of Shaphan was standing among them. Each had a censer in his hand, and a fragrant cloud of incense was rising.*

NIV Eze 8:12 *He said to me, "Son of man, have you seen what the elders of the house of Israel are doing in the darkness, each at the shrine of his own idol? They say, 'The LORD does not see us; the LORD has forsaken the land.'"*

NIV Eze 8:13 *Again, he said, "You will see them doing things that are even more detestable."*

NIV Eze 8:14 *Then he brought me to the entrance to the north gate of the house of the LORD, and I saw women sitting there, mourning for Tammuz.*

NIV Eze 8:15 *He said to me, "Do you see this, son of man? You will see things that are even more detestable than this."*

NIV Eze 8:16 *He then brought me into the inner court of the house of the LORD, and there at the entrance to the temple, between the portico and the altar, were about twenty-five men. With their backs toward the temple of the LORD and their faces toward the east, they were bowing down to the sun in the east.*

NIV Eze 8:17 *He said to me, "Have you seen this, son of man? Is it a trivial matter for the house of Judah to do the detestable things they are doing here? Must they also fill the land with violence and continually provoke me to anger? Look at them putting the branch to their nose!*

NIV Eze 8:18 *Therefore I will deal with them in anger; I will not look on them with pity or spare them. Although they shout in my ears, I will not listen to them."*

Here is the problem. We say we are worshiping our Savior as Christians on these holidays. However, which savior are we really celebrating? We believe we are worshiping the true Savior. However, we are practicing all of the rituals that are used to worship the other savior (according to Babylonian cult practices that were established long before Christ was born and even during the times of the Roman Empire).

Combine this with the fact that the Church is under a great deception, and that the gospel of the other savior is rising up within the ranks of the Church. We are confused! We are sleepwalking, yet God is telling us that this is no trivial matter! When both saviors are returned to us, will we suddenly not be confused and suddenly no longer be seduced by the other savior, who would save us from God's judgment by fighting Him?

You may think in your heart that you won't be confused. However, the Bible tells us something different. When everything we do surrounds the celebration of the antichrist, the other savior, and we follow his gospel of acceptance without conformity, mistaking it as unity, freedom, and forgiveness, then when he comes we will recognize him as our savior, because he will fit every image of how we understand the savior to be.

The "accepting" Church will gloat over the death of the two witnesses, disowning them as not from God. They, too, will be glad when Nimrod comes out of the temple from among the dead and kills them who were unkillable. They, too, will exchange gifts with each other, just as the world will do. However, they will have a rude awakening when they are destroyed by that other savior during the great tribulation.

Here is what David says about the futility of Nimrod's rebellion and his (supposed) salvation from Yahweh . This psalm is about the outcome of the battle of Armageddon.

NIV Psalm 2:

Why do the nations conspire and the peoples plot in vain? The kings of the earth take their stand and the rulers gather together against the LORD and against his Anointed One. "Let us break their chains," they say, "and throw off their fetters." The One enthroned in heaven laughs, the Lord scoffs at them. Then he rebukes them in his anger and terrifies them in his wrath, saying, "I have installed my King on Zion, my holy hill." I will proclaim the decree of the LORD: He said to me, "you are my Son, today I have become your Father, Ask of me, and I will make the nations your inheritance, the ends of the earth your possession. You will rule them with an iron scepter; you will dash them to pieces like pottery."

Therefore, you kings, be wise; he warned, you rulers of the earth. Serve the LORD with fear and rejoice with trembling. Kiss the Son, lest he be angry and you be destroyed in your way, for his wrath can flare up in a moment. Blessed are all who take refuge in him.

In reflection of the importance of what is about to transpire, we all, children of Adam, will be forced into making a choice: To serve self or to serve God. To follow the One Savior and live, or to follow the other savior who would attempt to save us from Yahweh, and then perish. Knowing all this, let us now soberly look once again at the departing words of Jesus, before He gave up His life in the body for our sake:

Amp Jn 14:15 *If you [really] love Me, you will keep (obey) My commands.*

Amp Jn 14:16 *And I will ask the Father, and He will give you another Comforter (Counselor, Helper, Intercessor, Advocate, Strengthener, and Standby), that He may remain with you forever—*

Amp Jn 14:17 *The Spirit of Truth, Whom the world cannot receive (welcome, take to its heart), because it does not see Him or know and recognize Him. But you know and recognize Him, for He lives with you [constantly] and will be in you.*

Amp Jn 14:18 *I will not leave you as orphans [comfortless, desolate, bereaved, forlorn, helpless]; I will come [back] to you.*

Amp Jn 14:19 *Just a little while now, and the world will not see Me any more, but you will see Me; because I live, you will live also.*

Amp Jn 14:20 *At that time [when that day comes] you will know [for yourselves] that I am in My Father, and you [are] in Me, and I [am] in you.*

Amp Jn 14:21 *The person who has My commands and keeps them is the one who [really] loves Me; and whoever [really] loves Me will be loved by My Father, and I [too] will love him and will show (reveal, manifest) Myself to him. [I will let Myself be clearly seen by him and make Myself real to him.]*

Amp Jn 14:22 *Judas, not Iscariot, asked Him, Lord, how is it that You will reveal Yourself [make Yourself real] to us and not to the world?*

Amp Jn 14:23 *Jesus answered, If a person [really] loves Me, he will keep My word [obey My teaching]; and My Father will love him, and We will come to him and make Our home (abode, special dwelling place) with him.*

Amp Jn 14:24 *Anyone who does not [really] love Me does not observe and obey My teaching. And the teaching which you hear and heed is not Mine, but [comes] from the Father Who sent Me.*

Amp Jn 14:25 *I have told you these things while I am still with you.*

Amp Jn 14:26 But the Comforter (Counselor, Helper, Intercessor, Advocate, Strengthener, Standby), the Holy Spirit, Whom the Father will send in My name [in My place, to represent Me and act on My behalf], He will teach you all things. And He will cause you to recall (will remind you of, bring to your remembrance) everything I have told you.

Amp Jn 14:27 Peace I leave with you; My [own] peace I now give and bequeath to you. Not as the world gives do I give to you. Do not let your hearts be troubled, neither let them be afraid. [Stop allowing yourselves to be agitated and disturbed; and do not permit yourselves to be fearful and intimidated and cowardly and unsettled.]

Amp Jn 14:28 You heard Me tell you, I am going away and I am coming [back] to you. If you [really] loved Me, you would have been glad, because I am going to the Father; for the Father is greater and mightier than I am.

Amp Jn 14:29 And now I have told you [this] before it occurs, so that when it does take place you may believe and have faith in and rely on Me.

Amp Jn 14:30 I will not talk with you much more, for the prince (evil genius, ruler) of the world is coming. And he has no claim on Me. [He has nothing in common with Me; there is nothing in Me that belongs to him, and he has no power over Me.]

Amp Jn 14:31 But [Satan is coming and] I do as the Father has commanded Me, so that the world may know (be convinced) that I love the Father and that I do only what the Father has instructed Me to do. [I act in full agreement with His orders.] Rise, let us go away from here.

Notes

[3] Flavius Josephus of the Antiquities of the Jews-Book 1. (n.d.). Retrieved September 2015, from penelope.uchicago.edu:penelope.uchicago.edu/josephus/ant-1.html

[4] Nimrod. (n.d.). Retrieved September 2015, from Jewish Encyclopedia: http://www.jewishencyclopedia.com/articles/11548-nimrod

[5] Nimrod. (n.d.). Retrieved September 2015, from Wikipedia: The Free Encyclopedia: https://en.wikipedia.org/wiki/Nimrod

[6] (n.d.). Kitāb Al-Magāll or The Book of the Rolls. In *One of the Books of Clement.* Retrieved from http://www.sacred-texts.com/chr/aa/aa2.htm

[7] Rogers, D. M. (2011, April). The Truth about Easter. Retrieved September 2015, from BibleTruth.cc: http://www.bibletruth.cc/Easter.htm#The_Ancient_Practice_of_the_40_Day_Fasting_and_Weeping

CHAPTER 6

The True Savior

^{NIV 1Co 15:35} *But someone may ask, "How are the dead raised? With what kind of body will they come?"*

^{NIV 1Co 15:36} *How foolish! What you sow does not come to life unless it dies.*

^{NIV 1Co 15:37} *When you sow, you do not plant the body that will be, but just a seed, perhaps of wheat or of something else.*

^{NIV 1Co 15:38} *But God gives it a body as he has determined, and to each kind of seed he gives its own body.*

^{NIV 1Co 15:39} *All flesh is not the same: Men have one kind of flesh, animals have another, birds another and fish another.*

^{NIV 1Co 15:40} *There are also heavenly bodies and there are earthly bodies; but the splendor of the heavenly bodies is one kind, and the splendor of the earthly bodies is another.*

NIV 1Co 15:41 *The sun has one kind of splendor, the moon another and the stars another; and star differs from star in splendor.*

NIV 1Co 15:42 *So will it be with the resurrection of the dead. The body that is sown is perishable, it is raised imperishable;*

NIV 1Co 15:43 *it is sown in dishonor, it is raised in glory; it is sown in weakness, it is raised in power;*

NIV 1Co 15:44 *it is sown a natural body, it is raised a spiritual body. If there is a natural body, there is also a spiritual body.*

NIV 1Co 15:45 *So it is written: "The first man Adam became a living being"; the last Adam, a life-giving spirit.*

NIV 1Co 15:46 *The spiritual did not come first, but the natural, and after that the spiritual.*

NIV 1Co 15:47 *The first man was of the dust of the earth, the second man from heaven.*

NIV 1Co 15:48 *As was the earthly man, so are those who are of the earth; and as is the man from heaven, so also are those who are of heaven.*

NIV 1Co 15:49 *And just as we have borne the likeness of the earthly man, so shall we bear the likeness of the man from heaven.*

NIV 1Co 15:50 *I declare to you, brothers, that flesh and blood cannot inherit the kingdom of God, nor does the perishable inherit the imperishable.*

Jesus and Nicodemus

NLT Jn 3:1 *After dark one evening, a Jewish religious leader named Nicodemus, a Pharisee,*

NLT Jn 3:2 *came to speak with Jesus. "Teacher," he said, "we all know that God has sent you to teach us. Your miraculous signs are proof enough that God is with you."*

NLT Jn 3:3 *Jesus replied, "I assure you, unless you are born again, you can never see the Kingdom of God."*

NLT Jn 3:4 *"What do you mean?" exclaimed Nicodemus. "How can an old man go back into his mother's womb and be born again?"*

NLT Jn 3:5 *Jesus replied, "The truth is, no one can enter the Kingdom of God without being born of water and the Spirit.*

NIV Jn 3:6 *Flesh gives birth to flesh, but the Spirit gives birth to spirit.*

NLT Jn 3:7 *So don't be surprised at my statement that you must be born again.*

NLT Jn 3:8 *Just as you can hear the wind but can't tell where it comes from or where it is going, so you can't explain how people are born of the Spirit."*

NLT Jn 3:9 *"What do you mean?" Nicodemus asked.*

NLT Jn 3:10 *Jesus replied, "You are a respected Jewish teacher, and yet you don't understand these things?*

NLT Jn 3:11 *I assure you, I am telling you what we know and have seen, and yet you won't believe us.*

NLT Jn 3:12 *But if you don't even believe me when I tell you about things that happen here on earth, how can you possibly believe if I tell you what is going on in heaven?*

NIV Jn 3:13 *No one has ever gone into heaven except the one who came from heaven— the Son of Man.*

NLT Jn 3:14 *And as Moses lifted up the bronze snake on a pole in the wilderness, so I, the Son of Man, must be lifted up on a pole,*

NLT Jn 3:15 *so that everyone who believes in me will have eternal life.*

NLT Jn 3:16 *"For God so loved the world that he gave his only Son, so that everyone who believes in him will not perish but have eternal life.*

NLT Jn 3:17 *God did not send his Son into the world to condemn it, but to save it.*

NLT Jn 3:18 *"There is no judgment awaiting those who trust him.*

NLT Jn 3:18 *But those who do not trust him have already been judged for not believing in the only Son of God.*

NLT Jn 3:19 *Their judgment is based on this fact: The light from heaven came into the world, but they loved the darkness more than the light, for their actions were evil.*

NLT Jn 3:20 *They hate the light because they want to sin in the darkness. They stay away from the light for fear their sins will be exposed and they will be punished.*

NLT Jn 3:21 *But those who do what is right come to the light gladly, so everyone can see that they are doing what God wants."*

Let us take a closer look at this famous dialogue Jesus had with Nicodemus in light of what was spoken of in 1 Corinthians:

NLT Jn 3:1 After dark one evening, a Jewish religious leader named Nicodemus, a Pharisee,

NLT Jn 3:2 came to speak with Jesus. "Teacher," he said, "we all know that God has sent you to teach us. Your miraculous signs are proof enough that God is with you."

NLT Jn 3:3 Jesus replied, "I assure you, unless you are born again, you can never see the Kingdom of God."

In saying, "unless you are born again, you can never see the Kingdom of God," Jesus is telling Nicodemus that, under the current circumstances, you will live and die and go disembodied into Hades, not to be raised from among the dead until the last day. And this will not happen until after the 1,000 year reign on earth (the Kingdom). As a result, you will not see My Kingdom or, in other words, be a part of it; you will be in Hades disembodied. However, if you are born again, you can be a part of My Kingdom (1,000 year reign).

NLT Jn 3:4 "What do you mean?" exclaimed Nicodemus. "How can an old man go back into his mother's womb and be born again?"

Nicodemus is obviously trying to understand Jesus' words in a natural sense and not a spiritual sense. This is understandable; after all, Jesus is talking to him about His Kingdom which is coming soon to the earth. However, they both are on the same wavelength when Nicodemus understands that when Jesus says, "born again," He is talking about a body by which to be clothed in. In other words, one needs to have a different body than he currently has in order to be a part of His Kingdom. However, Nicodemus' paradigm is earthbound, and, as such, only allows him to imagine in terms of another human body. Thus he would say, "How can a man be born when he is old? Can he enter his mother's womb again and be born?"

This is a very important point to understand in context to this conversation. We, thinking we are spiritual, may believe that Jesus is talking about being a spiritual creature in the sense that we in the spirit are born of God, as in a concept or an ideal, or as in an invisible nature. This thinking is like adopting someone as your son when he doesn't have your DNA, however, you embrace him as your own. It is true that to be born again, from Jesus' standpoint, means that our life-principle (spirit), which was that of the corrupt spirit of Adam we were born with, now needs to become His Spirit (life-principle).

However, in this conversation, Jesus is referring more towards a spiritual embodiment, meaning being clothed with a celestial body as opposed to a natural body. In other words, as a natural man with a natural body, our soul/personality must be born again, becoming a spiritual creature like that of an angel, having a spiritual or celestial body, and no longer being a natural creature with a natural body. We become a celestial human after being born of the spirit with a spiritual embodiment. In this case, it is like when you adopt someone as your son who doesn't have your DNA and there is a way to cause that same personality to be born again having a new body with your DNA (while discarding his old body). Then, he would become a true son. Understanding this in concept is why Nicodemus would say, "Can he enter his mother's womb again and be born?"

Jesus goes on to explain this in verses 5-7 below. In doing so, He first expounds on what He said about seeing the Kingdom of God by saying, "no one can enter the Kingdom of God without being born of water and the Spirit (as most translations say)." First, when it says, "born of water and the Spirit," the Greek word that is translated as "and" could be rendered also as "even" as the Amplified translation points out. In other words, it is better translated reflecting better context as saying without being born "of water, even the Spirit." Most people believe what Jesus is saying is that you have to undergo two baptisms, but actually He is talking about a rebirth, not a type of baptism. So, if it was rendered "of water, even the Spirit," water would simply be a metaphor for Spirit. So it is only talking about one rebirth, and not two baptisms.

Us knowing that there are two types of baptisms, one of water and one of Spirit, makes it easy for us to relate these words to baptism. However, at closer inspection, the word "baptism" is never actually used. It decidedly is talking about a rebirth of sorts. Here is what proves it; verse 6 clears it up. It says flesh gives birth to flesh, but the spirit gives birth to spirit.

In other words, in answer to your question, Nicodemus, your mother is a natural woman with a natural body. So naturally, she would give birth to you as a natural person. In order to be born a celestial being, having a body like that of an angel, you must be given birth from a spirit/celestial being. Therefore, gaining another embodiment wouldn't be by natural means. It wouldn't be through your natural mother's womb that you would attain a spiritual body.

Jesus goes on to say in verse 13 that He is the only one who has come down from heaven. In other words, He is a celestial being. In fact, He is the only celestial being who is one with God—who knows God. This qualifies Him to cause us to be reborn as a celestial being and, ultimately, possess a celestial body.

Let's look at the implications of that. We are talking about taking the soul of a man (which is the real man, his personality and the seat of rational and decision) away from being clothed as one type of creature and clothing him to become another kind of creature. We are born with the earthbound spirit of Adam, which is corrupt, and we have a natural body which consists of natural matter.

Jesus is in essence saying, I am going to give you a new Spirit, My Spirit, and I am going to give your soul, your personality, a new embodiment, which is spiritual in nature, consisting of spiritual matter. Our soul is going to transition from one dimension of reality to the next. Unlike going to outer space where we need to wear a spacesuit for our human body to survive, we will be given a completely different body that is natural to this new dimension that we will reside in—the coming Kingdom of God here on earth. This is the premise that Jesus has given us and is trying to help Nicodemus understand. This is nothing short of amazing!

One body will die within 100 years, the other will live forever. This being the case, therefore, we (meaning our mind and personality), being clothed with a completely new and different type of body made up of a different type of matter, will have to live in a different dimension from then on. From then on, we will no longer be creatures adapted to the natural universe. This is good, because God has already pronounced judgment on not only this earth, but this entire universe; it is going to be thrown into the lake of fire. Every element of matter that exists will melt and perish. However, we will not perish with it if our soul is no longer clothed with a body consisting of natural matter—we will go on for eternity.

This is God's solution so that He can bring an end to the world as He has judged, while still keeping His promise to Noah that He will not destroy everyone of the earth. The second judgment of water was the flood. Only eight people survived. However, they retained their human nature and their natural embodiment, which was corrupted by the first sin and the first judgment of death.

We started out by addressing Jesus' statement saying, "I assure you, most solemnly I tell you, unless a man is born of water, even the Spirit, he cannot ever enter the kingdom of God." Again, it is very important to understand the context of His words. And again, it is true that we can't enter into the Kingdom of God without being born of God's Spirit and no longer that of Adam's. However, what He is really referring to here is that you cannot enter into the Kingdom of God without possessing a celestial body. In other words, you can't enter into the Kingdom of God possessing a natural body. This is because the Kingdom of God is located in the spiritual realm, not in the natural realm. The spirit realm is not the habitat for a natural body.

The celestial city, the New Jerusalem, with its celestial creatures, including celestial humans, will come to the earth and cohabitate with mortal men on the natural earth. Even though (1) the Kingdom of Heaven comes within the celestial city, the New Jerusalem, and will be on the natural earth with mortal men, and (2) the celestial and the natural will interact with each other. The Kingdom that will rule the earth, nevertheless, will still be of one dimension while the earth is of another. As such, Jesus says that you shouldn't be surprised at Him saying that you need to be born of Spirit resulting in becoming a celestial human to enter into the Kingdom. Meaning: the New Jerusalem (the residence of Jesus, His Father, the angels, and celestial humans).

NLT Jn 3:5 *Jesus replied, "The truth is, no one can enter the Kingdom of God without being born of water and the Spirit.*
NIV Jn 3:6 *Flesh gives birth to flesh, but the Spirit gives birth to spirit.*
NLT Jn 3:7 *So don't be surprised at my statement that you must be born again.*

The Kingdom come is one of the biggest concepts that Jesus speaks about which is not fully understood by the majority of the Christian community. However, it is one of the most imperative things to understand. We could imagine that Jesus would say the same thing to all the Christian Church leaders today as He had said to Nicodemus back then; "You are a respected Jewish teacher, and yet you don't understand these things?" It is indeed pitiful that Church leaders do not understand the details or the context of what He is talking about here.

Any time in the New Testament when the term "the Kingdom of God" or "the Kingdom of Heaven," is used, it is talking about the Kingdom of Heaven coming to the earth. Meaning: the 1,000 year reign of Christ on earth in which He will rule the entire mortal world. Three Gospels use the term, Kingdom of God, however, Matthew refers to it as the Kingdom of Heaven. They are all referring to the same thing—God's Kingdom coming to rule the earth.

It only makes sense that the God of the universe, who is Spirit, would not come down to the earth and reside in the White House, or some penthouse apartment. That is because He is not a natural being. Of course, He would need to bring with Him accommodations, which consist of the natural habitat that He lives and functions in. That natural habitat is the New Jerusalem, a celestial city.

Now, it seems strange for Jesus to say, in essence, "You cannot see the Kingdom or enter into it unless you have a celestial body," considering the fact that He will come here on earth and He will rule all of the mortal people of the earth. Mortal people will be on the earth during His reign, otherwise, what is the point of reigning on earth, a planet in the natural universe? The following explains how both are true:

Jesus said to Pilate:

Amp Jn 18:36 ... *My kingdom (kingship, royal power) belongs not to this world. If My kingdom were of this world, My followers would have been fighting to keep Me from being handed over to the Jews. But as it is* (or "now" as other translations say), *My kingdom is not from here (this world); [it has no such origin or source].*

"As it is," or "now," leaves the opening that later His Kingdom will be a Kingdom over this world. However, the point is that His Kingdom origin is from a different realm, which is the spirit realm, or from heaven. We learn from Revelation that the city, "the New Jerusalem," will come from the spiritual realm and park itself on earth. Within those city walls is the habitation of God and His Son Jesus, the Christ.

This city is constructed of supernatural matter, not natural matter. The occupants of the city will be Jesus, the Father, the angels, and Jesus' bride of celestial human beings. It is from there, that they will minister to the nations and rule the earth for 1,000 years. They will rule the natural earth for 1,000 years, and mortal men will occupy the earth. But its government will be the government of the Messiah, who is a celestial being living in a celestial city. Somehow, the spiritual and the natural will be able to interact with each other during this time period.

Therefore, when Jesus says you will not be able to see (be a part of) the Kingdom of God, nor will you be able to enter into the Kingdom of God unless you are born of Spirit and then possess an immortal or celestial body, He is saying that you cannot enter into the New Jerusalem unless you have a celestial body. Apparently, celestial beings will be able to manifest and interact with mortal men in the natural world.

On the other hand, it does not work the same way for mortal men. Mortal men, even disembodied men in Hades will not be able to manifest and interact in the celestial city, the New Jerusalem. This is because it is a city made of supernatural matter. He is also saying to Nicodemus that you will not be able to be a part of His reign on the earth (or see it) because it is thousands of years from now, and you will be dead, disembodied, waiting in Hades until after His reign. At which time, on the last day, you will finally be resurrected and once again be clothed with a body.

However, by then it will be too late to have taken part in My Kingdom (on earth). It will have had its time, but you will still have an opportunity to live in it and be a part of eternity, depending on how you are judged on the last day—a sheep or a goat. At that point, you will be among those who were first (the Israelites), but you are last because of your unbelief. And others who get their celestial bodies by being born again will be the last who became first before you, because of their belief in the Son of God. Conversely, if you become born again of a new Spirit and attain your celestial body, you too can live with Me in the New Jerusalem and be a part of My 1,000 year reign, not having to wait until the last day.

Note: This clears something up. The majority of Christians believe that if we miss the opportunity to be a part of the Kingdom of God, the 1,000 year reign of Christ, then we will go to hell for eternity, believing it is either one or the other. This is a huge misnomer! If you have a New Covenant relationship with Jesus, you will not taste death, and you will be a part of His 1,000 year reign. It is by your relationship with Him that you make this group.

Secondly, those who endure the great tribulation and the outpouring of God's wrath on the world (two separate but back-to-back time periods) can take part in the first resurrection and still be a part of His 1,000 year reign. It is due to their profession that this group makes it. If they do not denounce their testimony and do not worship the beast, nor receive his mark, then they will, by profession, make this group.

A person, even a Christian (just as with the Israelites) can find themselves unable to qualify to be a part of the Kingdom of God as a celestial being during the 1,000 year reign. That's correct, even Christians (like the Israelites) can be a part of the group that is last and not first, when it comes to entering into eternity. The group that is first are those who gain their celestial body and are a part of the 1,000 year reign. The group that is last are those who remain disembodied in Hades until the last day, after the 1,000 year reign, and will then be found worthy to be a part of eternity when they are judged. They will die a normal death, become disembodied, have their soul assigned to Hades, and await the last day, at which time they will be resurrected and clothed in bodily form once again.

This third group will be judged by their deeds—how they had conducted themselves during their lives. They will, at that time, either be condemned and thrown alive into the lake of fire for all of eternity enduring yet a second death, or they will, because of their deeds, be deemed acceptable by God. Jesus tells us that the minimum requirement to enter into eternity on the judgment day is if you have so much as given a cup of cold water to the most immature Christian that was in union with Him while they were in their mortal body on the earth (Mat 10:41-42). These (considered sheep) will, therefore, go on living for all of eternity with Jesus, the bride, and the angels in the city, the New Jerusalem. At that point, the New Jerusalem will relocate to a new earth in a new universe which is in the supernatural realm.

Through Jesus' redemption, we can circumvent judgment on the last day and thereby avoid facing the prospects of a second death, and also be exempt from ever experiencing death (disembodiment of the soul). Instead, we will rule the entire earth with Jesus, clothed with a celestial body like that of the angels. These are the advantages of having a New Covenant relationship with Jesus. We no longer have to go through the "rite-of-passage" that all of the human race has no choice but to go through in order to possibly attain life eternal.

That "rite-of-passage" is to die and become a disembodied soul held captive in Hades until the last day. After that, we will be resurrected and reclothed with a body so that we may face the day of judgment on that last day. Finally, we will be judged by God as suitable or not to go on living for eternity. If not, then we will be found deserving to suffer a second death by being thrown alive into the lake of fire.

A New Covenant relationship with Jesus will exempt us from going through what every single human has been cursed with (death— disembodiment of the soul). However, it is imperative to recognize that qualifying for this group has nothing to do with your profession or your deeds, no matter how great they are. What qualifies you to be a part of the Kingdom of God on the earth is your relationship with Jesus. A relationship which makes the two of you one, in union with each other.

This is why Jesus says many will complain, saying it is unfair because they did so many good deeds and supported His Kingdom work (according to their own inspiration), but yet he rejects them from being a part of this group stating, "I never knew you." Meaning, I never had a New Covenant relationship of union with you.

Understanding these facts will also clear up a great deal of seeming discrepancies between the Old Testament and the New Testament. When it comes to prophetic words given about the coming 1,000 year Kingdom of the Christ here on mortal earth, there are so many points where the two seem to not agree with each other.

These differences can be cleared up by the exact clarity Jesus is trying to give Nicodemus between the two different realms. For the most part, Old Testament prophecy speaks about the 1,000 year reign of the Messiah from a mortal or natural standpoint. Conversely, New Testament prophecy speaks of the 1,000 year reign of Christ from a celestial, spiritual, or heavenly standpoint. Let's give an example:

The Two Cities:

Old Testament: The Gates of the City

NIV Eze 48:30 *"These will be the exits of the city: Beginning on the north side, which is 4,500 cubits long* (1.25 miles),

NIV Eze 48:31 *the gates of the city will be named after the tribes of Israel. The three gates on the north side will be the gate of Reuben, the gate of Judah and the gate of Levi.*

NIV Eze 48:32 *"On the east side, which is 4,500 cubits long, will be three gates: the gate of Joseph, the gate of Benjamin and the gate of Dan.*

NIV Eze 48:33 *"On the south side, which measures 4,500 cubits, will be three gates: the gate of Simeon, the gate of Issachar and the gate of Zebulun.*

NIV Eze 48:34 *"On the west side, which is 4,500 cubits long, will be three gates: the gate of Gad, the gate of Asher and the gate of Naphtali.*

NIV Eze 48:35 *"The distance all around will be 18,000 cubits* (5 miles circumference or 1.6 square miles). *"And the name of the city from that time on will be:*

THE LORD IS THERE. "

Ezekiel speaks prophetically of the 1,000 year reign of the Messiah. He tells us that there will be a city there called, "THE LORD IS THERE," presumably where Jerusalem currently exists. In this city, there will be a temple where there will be sacrifices made to the Lord. The Prince of the city will have a room within that temple that the presence of the Lord will be in, and He will eat the sacrificed meal with God's presence there in fellowship.

In the New Testament book of Revelation, John tells us that there will be a city there in the same place called, "the New Jerusalem." It is the residence and court of the Father and His Son in heaven. It was constructed in heaven on a huge hill. It is a celestial city. John goes on to say that it comes down to the earth with that hill underneath it and rests where Old Jerusalem is now. Are we talking about the same city described by two different prophets who don't agree? Or, are they two different cities? How is that possible that you have two cities in the same location? Ezekiel tells us that in the city called THE LORD IS THERE, there is a temple and sacrifices are made. However, John tells us that in the New Jerusalem there is no temple, the Father and Jesus are the temple. He also says that the light of God shining from within the New Jerusalem will replace the sun and the moon as a source of light for the whole earth.

NIV Rev 21:22 *I did not see a temple in the city, because the Lord God Almighty and the Lamb are its temple.*

NIV Rev 21:23 *The city does not need the sun or the moon to shine on it, for the glory of God gives it light, and the Lamb is its lamp.*

NIV Rev 21:24 *The nations will walk by its light, and the kings of the earth will bring their splendor into it.*

NIV Rev 21:25 *On no day will its gates ever be shut, for there will be no night there.*

NIV Rev 21:26 *The glory and honor of the nations will be brought into it.*

NIV Rev 21:27 *Nothing impure will ever enter it, nor will anyone who does what is shameful or deceitful, but only those whose names are written in the Lamb's book of life.*

Here is another problem. Israel is between the Mediterranean Sea on one side and the Dead Sea on the other. It consists of 8,019 square miles of land. At its widest point, it is 71 miles, and at its narrowest point, it is only 9 miles wide. The New Jerusalem, according to John, consists of 2,560,000 square miles. This is the size of the mainland of the United States minus several of its states. On the other hand, Ezekiel's city named, "THE LORD IS THERE," is a city the size of approximately 1.6 square miles. This city will fit neatly where Jerusalem exists now.

The question is, how can you fit a city that is 320 times larger than the land underneath it? Additionally, how can we reconcile the difference between Ezekiel's city with a temple and John's New Jerusalem without a temple? In addition, the New Jerusalem comes with its own hill underneath it. Again, a hill almost the size of the United States mainland at the top where the city sits. One can only guess how big it is at the base of the hill.

The answer is: one city exists in one realm, and the other city exists in the other realm. Although they may occupy the same space, they are obviously in two separate dimensions. We see how Ezekiel and John's versions come together when the angel that was helping Ezekiel measure the temple points out to Ezekiel that there is a water leak of sorts coming into the temple. That water leak, when followed, turns into a stream. As they follow it further, it widens into a river that runs all the way to the Dead Sea. On each side of the river, it is teeming with life, including fruit trees that bear fruit monthly instead of annually. Ezekiel tells us that when the river empties into the Dead Sea, it causes the Dead Sea to come alive and produce all kinds of fish and life for the fishermen who gather there.

NIV Rev 21:27 *Nothing impure will ever enter it, nor will anyone who does what is shameful or deceitful, but only those whose names are written in the Lamb's book of life.*

Here is another important thing to point out. In verse 27 (above) it says only those whose names are written in the Lamb's book of life can enter into the city, the New Jerusalem. Who are those who have been written in the Lamb's book of life? The answer is, the redeemed of Jesus, His bride, the last who enter into eternity before the first. This includes:

(1) The 144,000 disembodied Israelites who became clothed in their celestial bodies and were able to leave Hades as the prisoners who were set free by Jesus when He died on the cross.

(2) Those people who are in union with Jesus—those who have a New Covenant relationship with Him. The ones who, upon their death, do not become disembodied but are clothed with a celestial body and are in heaven even before their heads hit the ground in death (*The Church Pure*). This includes those who will be raptured at the onset of the great tribulation, and again, will not experience death.

(3) Lastly, the participants of the first resurrection after the great tribulation, along with the survivors who held fast to their testimonies of Jesus, who did not worship the beast, or receive his mark.

All three groups will be celestial humans and no longer natural humans. They will be as the angels whose natural habitat is the spirit realm. These are those who are written in the Lamb's book of life and consequently will be His bride in the New Jerusalem having celestial bodies, ruling with Jesus as kings and priests for 1,000 years on earth even before the last day.

The balance of people who will enter into the eternity of the new heavens and the new earth will do so after the 1,000 year reign of Christ, and after the last day when all will be resurrected and judged. If they are not sentenced to the second death (the lake of fire), they will be considered sheep and allowed to be part of eternity. Among these people are:

(1) Those who Jesus spoke about when He said, "Many who are first will be last." Meaning, the people of God, the Israelites, who knew God, yet, did not believe that Jesus was their Messiah. They are the first who do not get to take part in His Kingdom on earth, as previously discussed. However, the Israelites who are alive as mortal humans during the time of His Kingdom will have a very special status, the rest of the world will serve them and their nation. In spite of this special status while alive, they will go the way of the Israelites who have died in days gone by. They will go to the paradisiacal place in Hades as disembodied souls and

await the last day when they will be resurrected, face judgment, and hopefully be declared sheep. As Jesus told them, they will have to wait until the last day before entering in.

(2) Those who are judged on the last day by their deeds and are found acceptable.

(3) Those who were kind, even giving as little as a glass of cold water to the redeemed of Christ while they lived in the body on earth. Jesus promised of them that they would surely not lose their reward (like: any friend of My children are a friend of Mine). All of this agrees with what Jesus told Nicodemus in the verses above.

Here is one more set of verses that refers to the New Jerusalem and its occupants:

Amp Jn 12:24 *I assure you, most solemnly I tell you, Unless a grain of wheat falls into the earth and dies, it remains [just one grain; it never becomes more but lives] by itself alone. But if it dies, it produces many others and yields a rich harvest.*
Amp Jn 12:25 *Anyone who loves his life loses it, but anyone who hates his life in this world will keep it to life eternal. [Whoever has no love for, no concern for, no regard for his life here on earth, but despises it, preserves his life forever and ever.]*
Amp Jn 12:26 *If anyone serves Me, he must continue to follow Me [to cleave steadfastly to Me, conform wholly to My example in living and, if need be, in dying] and wherever I am, there will My servant be also. If anyone serves Me, the Father will honor him.*

Jesus is referring to His future Kingdom here on earth. He is reasoning that if He doesn't die, then His Spirit will not be poured out into the world, and His followers will not be able to come into spiritual union with Him as a result. In this case, when He comes into His Kingdom here on earth, it will be Jesus, His Father, and His angels who will occupy the New Jerusalem and rule the inhabitants of the earth, the mortal men, for 1,000 years. This is what He means when He relates Himself to a grain of wheat, saying that if it doesn't die, it will remain "alone." This is a strange statement if you consider that He will be ruling all of the mortal men of the earth, including His precious people Israel, during His 1,000 year reign. He will have His Father, the angels, and all of His subjects—the mortal men of the earth. How, then, can He say He will be alone?

However, in context to what He told Nicodemus, Jesus is really saying by verses 25-26: When I come into My Kingdom on earth and reign for 1,000 years, I don't want to be alone in that I have no fellowship with men in My New Jerusalem where I will reside and rule from. Because none of them will gain a celestial body if I don't die. As a result, during My 1,000 year reign and in My city, the New Jerusalem, I will be alone in My court, even though I will rule all the mortal men of the earth, including My people, the (mortal) Israelites in their land, which I will restore to them.

Mortal men will either be on the natural earth in mortal bodies unable to enter into the New Jerusalem, or they will be disembodied in Hades (dead) waiting for the last day after My reign, when they will be resurrected and finally receive their celestial body, or go the way of the second death. However, if I die, then many will be redeemed and receive a celestial body. I will then have those in spiritual union with Me, My bride. I will not be alone in My court! My bride, celestial humans, will fill My court and see Me face to face. I will give them authority over the nations of the earth. They will rule with Me over the mortal men of the earth during My Millennium Reign from My celestial city, the New Jerusalem.

NIV Rev 2:26 To him who overcomes and does my will to the end, I will give authority over the nations

NIV Rev 22:3 . . . The throne of God and of the Lamb will be in the city, and his servants will serve him.

NIV Rev 22:4 They will see his face, and his name will be on their foreheads.

Where is this water leaking from?

The River From the Temple

NIV Eze 47:1 The man brought me back to the entrance of the temple, and I saw water coming out from under the threshold of the temple toward the east (for the temple faced east). The water was coming down from under the south side of the temple, south of the altar.

NIV Eze 47:2 He then brought me out through the north gate and led me around the outside to the outer gate facing east, and the water was flowing from the south side.

NIV Eze 47:3 As the man went eastward with a measuring line in his hand, he measured off a thousand cubits and then led me through water that was ankle-deep.

NIV Eze 47:4 He measured off another thousand cubits and led me through water that was knee-deep. He measured off another thousand and led me through water that was up to the waist.

NIV Eze 47:5 He measured off another thousand, but now it was a river that I could not cross, because the water had risen and was deep enough to swim in—a river that no one could cross.

NIV Eze 47:6 He asked me, "Son of man, do you see this?" Then he led me back to the bank of the river.

NIV Eze 47:7 When I arrived there, I saw a great number of trees on each side of the river.

NIV Eze 47:8 He said to me, "This water flows toward the eastern region and goes down into the Arabah, where it enters the Sea (the Dead Sea). When it empties into the Sea, the water there becomes fresh.

NIV Eze 47:9 Swarms of living creatures will live wherever the river flows. There will be large numbers of fish, because this water flows there and makes the salt water fresh; so where the river flows everything will live.

NIV Eze 47:10 Fishermen will stand along the shore; from En Gedi to En Eglaim there will be places for spreading nets. The fish will be of many kinds —like the fish of the Great Sea (the Mediterranean Sea).

NIV Eze 47:11 But the swamps and marshes will not become fresh; they will be left for salt.

NIV Eze 47:12 Fruit trees of all kinds will grow on both banks of the river. Their leaves will not wither, nor will their fruit fail. Every month they will bear, because the water from the sanctuary flows to them. Their fruit will serve for food and their leaves for healing.

John tells us about the river of life that runs down the center of the New Jerusalem, with the tree of life growing on both sides of it. The celestial humans (the bride of Christ) will use and distribute its leaves to heal the nations. And it says that all the mortal people of the earth will be free to drink from the waters of the river of life.

The River of Life

NIV Rev 22:1 Then the angel showed me the river of the water of life, as clear as crystal, flowing from the throne of God and of the Lamb

NIV Rev 22:2 down the middle of the great street of the city. On each side of the river stood the tree of life, bearing twelve crops of fruit, yielding its fruit every month. And the leaves of the tree are for the healing of the nations.

NIV Rev 22:3 No longer will there be any curse. The throne of God and of the Lamb will be in the city, and his servants will serve him.

NIV Rev 22:4 They will see his face, and his name will be on their foreheads.

NIV Rev 22:5 There will be no more night. They will not need the light of a lamp or the light of the sun, for the Lord God will give them light. And they will reign for ever and ever.

This river somehow trickles down from the supernatural city of the New Jerusalem and manifests into drinkable water for mortals on the earth, resulting in a river in the natural world. It flows from the New Jerusalem and at the same time from outside the temple in the city, THE LORD IS THERE, to the Dead Sea. Obviously Ezekiel and John sound like they don't agree with each other.

This discrepancy is resolved if you consider one is prophesying about the same geographic place and time period as the other having as context the following: One is doing so from the perspective of the spiritual dimension, while the other is doing so from the perspective of the natural or mortal world. Having the context of the two prophets speaking of the same thing, only in two different dimensions, helps us reconcile why they don't match up perfectly.

Likewise, Jesus explained to Nicodemus that you need to be born again, resulting in being clothed with a celestial body and no longer that of a natural body. This will allow you to be a part of the Millennium Reign, and most importantly, enter into the New Jerusalem. Therefore, you will be able to enter into the Kingdom of God/heaven—a celestial city.

Now to finish up the teaching Jesus was speaking to Nicodemus:

NLT Jn 3:8 Just as you can hear the wind but can't tell where it comes from or where it is going, so you can't explain how people are born of the Spirit."
NLT Jn 3:9 "What do you mean?" Nicodemus asked.

NLT Jn 3:10 Jesus replied, *"You are a respected Jewish teacher, and yet you don't understand these things?*

NLT Jn 3:11 *I assure you, I am telling you what we know and have seen, and yet you won't believe us.*

NLT Jn 3:12 *But if you don't even believe me when I tell you about things that happen here on earth, how can you possibly believe if I tell you what is going on in heaven?*

Again (above), Jesus is trying to communicate that there is another dimension, the spiritual dimension, which is a big part of the future of the world and especially His coming Kingdom to the earth. Trying to get them to think in terms of that additional aspect of His reign proves difficult for Him as He tries to get people to expand their perception to include the celestial or heavenly role in His coming Kingdom.

As mentioned, the Old Testament prophets spoke visions of the coming Kingdom primarily in the perspective of the natural or mortal world. They saw the Kingdom coming and it's Messiah as a child of David who was part of the natural world and who would war against the entire world on behalf of Israel. Jesus defeating all the nations, not only will bring peace and security to Israel for a thousand years, but will cause all the governments of the nations to serve Israel. After that, somehow His kingdom will spill into eternity.

Here is an interesting observation. Currently in the Gospel age of these New Testament times, the contemporary Church has difficulty relating to the natural or mortal aspect of Jesus' coming Kingdom. We think only in terms of either going to heaven or, if we miss the boat, going to hell. It is rarely factored in that Jesus will be on earth for 1,000 years. It is also not common knowledge that Jesus' redemption is to recruit celestial humans who would rule with Him for 1,000 years before the end. Neither is it considered that if you miss out on that chance, you can still make it to heaven on the last day. In fact, we in modern times don't understand that when Jesus spoke, He spoke more about the coming Kingdom of God here on earth for 1,000 years than He spoke about other subjects.

If you qualify for being a part of His Kingdom, you already possess life eternal. If you put things in perspective, you realize the significance of Him instructing the disciples to proclaim that the Kingdom of Heaven is near. It was said of John the Baptist that he preached, "Repent, for the Kingdom of Heaven is near."

The cry of John the Baptist:

NIV Mt 3:1 *In those days John the Baptist came, preaching in the Desert of Judea* *NIV Mt 3:2* *and saying, "Repent, for the kingdom of heaven is near."*

What Jesus preached:

NIV Mt 4:17 *From that time on Jesus began to preach, "Repent, for the kingdom of heaven is near."*

What Jesus taught His disciples to preach:

NIV Mt 10:5 *These twelve Jesus sent out with the following instructions: "Do not go among the Gentiles or enter any town of the Samaritans.* *NIV Mt 10:6* *Go rather to the lost sheep of Israel.* *NIV Mt 10:7* *As you go, preach this message: 'The kingdom of heaven is near.'*

What the people of Israel understood by the preaching of, "the Kingdom of heaven is near," is not what we understand today. What they understood was that their Messiah was coming soon, and He would put all things right; all the enemies of Israel would be destroyed, and all the nations would be in servitude to Israel for 1,000 years in the mortal world. Indeed, this is exactly what Jesus was trying to communicate. However, and at the same time, Jesus was giving us a more full picture of what that looks like—that the supernatural and the natural will cohabitate. The supernatural city, the New Jerusalem, where the celestial beings of heaven reside, will come to the earth and rule over it on behalf of the mortals of the nation of Israel.

So when He makes a statement like, when it's time for the wedding banquet, those who are not wearing wedding clothes (meaning those not clothed with a celestial body) will be thrown outside where there will be darkness, weeping, wailing, and gnashing of teeth, He is referring to the New Jerusalem and the great tribulation. The New Jerusalem, being a celestial city, requires a celestial body to enter. In that city, there will be bliss and a celebration between Jesus and those who are in spiritual union with Him—His bride. Conversely, outside the city mortal men will be reeling and staggering under the outpouring of God's wrath in the natural earth, where darkness and torment prevail just before His reign takes over the mortal world. As stated previously, somehow both places will occupy the same space, only within different dimensions.

NIV Mt 22:8 *"Then he said to his servants, 'The wedding banquet is ready, but those I invited did not deserve to come.*

NIV Mt 22:9 *Go to the street corners and invite to the banquet anyone you find.'*

NIV Mt 22:10 *So the servants went out into the streets and gathered all the people they could find, both good and bad, and the wedding hall was filled with guests.*

NIV Mt 22:11 *"But when the king came in to see the guests, he noticed a man there who was not wearing wedding clothes.*

NIV Mt 22:12 *'Friend,' he asked, 'how did you get in here without wedding clothes?' The man was speechless.*

NIV Mt 22:13 *"Then the king told the attendants, 'Tie him hand and foot, and throw him outside, into the darkness, where there will be weeping and gnashing of teeth.'*

NIV Mt 22:14 *"For many are invited, but few are chosen."*

It is important to recognize that when Jesus came here the first time, it was not just to die so that we would not have to experience death, but also to recruit mortal men, convincing them to exchange their short lives in the flesh (in this world) for a life in the coming Kingdom. This life will be one in which their celestial bodies will live forever, rule with Him, and will not be subject to sickness, death, pain, exhausting labor, the heat and cold of the weather, hunger, nor thirst. Those who give up their lives by living for the Spirit of God in exchange for their own goals, agendas, and desires are visionaries, living for the future. The people of the world who squirrel up nuts for the winter and money for retirement are considered wise and forward thinkers. However, it is a greater wisdom to hate your life in the flesh, exchanging it for a celestial body, and live to be with Jesus in the Kingdom to come.

Continuing with Jesus and Nicodemus:

NIV Jn 3:13 No one has ever gone into heaven except the one who came from heaven— the Son of Man.

NLT Jn 3:14 And as Moses lifted up the bronze snake on a pole in the wilderness, so I, the Son of Man, must be lifted up on a pole,

NLT Jn 3:15 so that everyone who believes in me will have eternal life.

NLT Jn 3:16 "For God so loved the world that he gave his only Son, so that everyone who believes in him will not perish but have eternal life.

NLT Jn 3:17 God did not send his Son into the world to condemn it, but to save it.

NLT Jn 3:18 "There is no judgment awaiting those who trust him. . .

In another place Jesus says:

Amp Jn 8:51 I assure you, most solemnly I tell you, if anyone observes My teaching [lives in accordance with My message, keeps My word], he will by no means ever see and experience death.

Amp Jn 8:52 *The Jews said to Him, Now we know that You are under the power of a demon (insane). Abraham died, and also the prophets, yet You say, If a man keeps My word, he will never taste of death into all eternity.*

Amp Jn 8:53 *Are You greater than our father Abraham? He died, and all the prophets died! Who do You make Yourself out to be?*

How does it become true when it is said, "Jesus died for me"?

Furthermore, is it literal when Jesus said that those who believe Him will never die? How does this work when clearly every Christian since Jesus walked the earth has died when their time came?

In order to answer the first question, we must answer the last two questions first. This is how it works: before our head hits the ground in death, we are already before His throne, in a celestial body, avoiding the experience of actually dying or becoming disembodied. The account of the stoning of Stephen helps us see how this is true. Stephen's soul was being taken up to heaven, to his celestial body before the Lord, even before the people took him out to the street to stone him. His soul was not even in his body when he was being stoned. He was alive in another body in heaven even before his physical body fell. His physical body was literally like a chicken running around with its head cut off. His body died, but he was clothed in a different body before the life was no longer able to animate his previous body, therefore, he did not experience death—to be disembodied.

NIV Ac 7:54 *When they heard this, they were furious and gnashed their teeth at him.*

NIV Ac 7:55 *But Stephen, full of the Holy Spirit, looked up to heaven and saw the glory of God, and Jesus standing at the right hand of God.*

NIV Ac 7:56 *"Look," he said, "I see heaven open and the Son of Man standing at the right hand of God."*

NIV Ac 7:57 *At this they covered their ears and, yelling at the top of their voices, they all rushed at him,*

NIV Ac 7:58 *dragged him out of the city and began to stone him.*

Amp Jn 14:20 *At that time [when that day comes] you will know [for yourselves] that I am in My Father, and you [are] in Me, and I [am] in you.*

When the people of the earth watch your body fall to the ground, they think of you as having died. You, on the other hand, find yourself clothed in a celestial body before the throne of God, even before your physical body goes into the throes of death. Therefore, Jesus is made true when He says whoever obeys His teachings will never die and will avoid judgment; they already possess eternal life.

Amp Jn 11:25 *Jesus said to her, I am [Myself] the Resurrection and the Life. Whoever believes in (adheres to, trusts in, and relies on) Me, although he may die, yet he shall live;*
Amp Jn 11:26 *And whoever continues to live and believes in Me shall never [actually] die at all. Do you believe this?*

Amp Jn 5:24 *I assure you, most solemnly I tell you, the person whose ears are open to My words [who listens to My message] and believes and trusts in and clings to and relies on Him Who sent Me has (possesses now) eternal life. And he does not come into judgment [does not incur sentence of judgment, will not come under condemnation], but he has already passed over out of death into life.*

Those whose bodies die before the return of Jesus will transition from life to life as described above. That is, if they are those who have died to their own life and live by every prompting of His Spirit in them. Jesus died for this very purpose. Those in that group, who are alive, living in their mortal bodies when the day the great tribulation begins, will, like Stephen, be raised to heaven to a new celestial body in a twinkling of an eye, even before they can comprehend what happened. This is what Jesus was talking about when He said:

NIV Jn 14:20 *On that day you will realize that I am in my Father, and you are in me, and I am in you.*

The day Jesus is referring to is the day you will be lifted up to heaven because His Spirit in you has lifted you up. And by that you will realize that He is in His Father, and you are in Him and He is in you. That day is the day of the rapture. It is also the day that He will vomit the *Church Corrupt* out of His mouth and withdraw His Spirit (along with those who live by His Spirit) from the earth, abandoning her to the darkness of the desolation—the great tribulation. This will be the time of the beast. He (the beast/antichrist) will kill the elect Jesus leaves behind, because His Spirit was not found in them. They will taste death, and go to Hades, disembodied.

However, those who stand firm to their testimony will rise in the first resurrection. This resurrection is, in fact, exclusively for them, and no others. The rest will wait until the last day, some 1,000 years after the return of Christ, and then be resurrected and judged either as sheep or goats. The latter will be thrown alive into the lake of fire for eternity, suffering a second death after having just been resurrected from being disembodied for the purpose of being judged. The former will be granted eternal life.

Although His substitutionary death was offered for all, He did not die for everyone. Who is it that can say, "Jesus died for me"? That is the real question. The answer is more simple than you would think. It is those who did not and do not have to experience death, not even once. When all is said and done, these are the ones who Jesus died for, the ones who do not die ever. For the others He saves, His substitutionary death allows them to be set free from the disembodiment of death, and gain a celestial body in order to live for eternity. They will die, but at one time or another come alive again with a new incorruptible body. However, they will suffer and know the sting of death.

The truth is, Jesus died and became disembodied so that those who believe in Him do not have to experience death. The one thing God has never had to do is experience death, because He's God. However, out of love, He did the unthinkable and gave Himself over to death so that we who are doomed to death would not have to experience it. He broke open His earthen vessel, and His Spirit spilled out into the earth, disembodied. Those who choose to embody His Spirit (not just to house it like the man who buried the one talent given to him) but to give expression to His Spirit through their bodies collectively—are the body of Christ in the world, His bride, His Church. Together, the two have become one flesh (one whole person).

NIV Jn 19:33 *But when they came to Jesus and found that he was already dead, they did not break his legs.*

NIV Jn 19:34 *Instead, one of the soldiers pierced Jesus' side with a spear, bringing a sudden flow of blood and water.*

What makes this event significant—the blood and water flowing out of Jesus' body and spilling out onto the earth—is that it is a representation of how the Spirit of Christ became disembodied in the earth through His death. For it says, the life (spirit) is in the blood. In addition, it says that His spilled blood cries out a much finer thing than that of Abel.

NLT Heb 12:24 *You have come to Jesus, the one who mediates the new covenant between God and people, and to the sprinkled blood, which graciously forgives instead of crying out for vengeance as the blood of Abel did.*

Because Jesus remains in the earth to this very day as a disembodied Spirit, having lost, even sacrificed His mortal body, we who have a natural body, can become one flesh with Him through the binding of ourselves to His living and active Spirit.

This is how it works: Jesus dies to His body and we die to our lives in the body. He says, "If you love Me, you will obey what I command." The meaning of this saying goes way beyond simply showing love by being loyal and obedient. No deeper union can be attained between two people than making the two one. If the one soul with a body voluntarily, out of love, obeys the Spirit of the other soul who has no body in the earth—giving expression to the will of the other through his body—then the two become one whole person. There is no other type of union or marriage that is more binding or intimate than this, which makes the two become one. Not even physical sex can produce the ecstasy and oneness that spiritual union can produce when the two, together, become one whole person.

NAS GAL 2:20 *"I have been crucified with Christ; and it is no longer I who live, but Christ lives in me; and the life which I now live in the flesh I live by faith in the Son of God, who loved me and gave Himself up for me.*
NAS GAL 2:21 *"I do not nullify the grace of God, for if righteousness comes through the Law, then Christ died needlessly."*

NIV Ro 12:1 *Therefore, I urge you, brothers, in view of God's mercy, to offer your bodies as living sacrifices, holy and pleasing to God—this is your spiritual act of worship.*

NIV 1Co 6:17 *But he who unites himself with the Lord is one with him in spirit.*

Jesus Prays for All Believers

NIV Jn 17:20 *"My prayer is not for them alone. I pray also for those who will believe in me through their message,*
NIV Jn 17:21 *that all of them may be one, Father, just as you are in me and I am in you. May they also be in us so that the world may believe that you have sent me.*
NIV Jn 17:22 *I have given them the glory that you gave me, that they may be one as we are one:*
NIV Jn 17:23 *I in them and you in me. May they be brought to complete unity to let the world know that you sent me and have loved them even as you have loved me.*

NIV Jn 17:24 "Father, I want those you have given me to be with me where I am, and to see my glory, the glory you have given me because you loved me before the creation of the world.

NIV Jn 17:25 "Righteous Father, though the world does not know you, I know you, and they know that you have sent me.

NIV Jn 17:26 I have made you known to them, and will continue to make you known in order that the love you have for me may be in them and that I myself may be in them."

By His death on the cross, Jesus makes a way for Himself to have fellowship with celestial humans in His celestial city while He rules mortal humans on the natural earth for 1,000 years. To those who are celestial humans, He will not just be a powerful presence as He will to the mortals in the earth, but they will know His form and fellowship directly with Him, face-to-face, in His celestial city, the New Jerusalem.

Amp Rev 22:3 There shall no longer exist there anything that is accursed (detestable, foul, offensive, impure, hateful, or horrible). But the throne of God and of the Lamb shall be in it, and His servants shall worship Him [pay divine honors to Him and do Him holy service].

Amp Rev 22:4 They shall see His face, and His name shall be on their foreheads.

Amp Rev 22:5 And there shall be no more night; they have no need for lamplight or sunlight, for the Lord God will illuminate them and be their light, and they shall reign [as kings] forever and ever (through the eternities of the eternities).

CHAPTER 7

The Judgment of Fire

The judgment of fire is the third and final judgment, that will take us to the end. This judgment has already started; it began a couple of generations after the flood. Whether you know it or are ignorant of it, whether you believe it or do not believe it, whether you conduct your life in light of its implications or you ignore the storms we live in and the doom we are headed for, it doesn't matter; it is a fact! There is only one outcome, and it is falling on all of us, without exception. But there is a way out, and it is not by human strength or wit!

We will tell the story of the judgment of fire through the accounts of the 7 seals and of the 70-7's in the Bible. This will bring a conclusion to *The Christian Story and its Message*.

The story of the judgment of fire starts at the beginning, the new beginning. It starts with the eight people who survived the flood. We have already shown the origins of the judgment of fire in the chapter about Nimrod, the beast and antichrist. Even before the ark hit dry land, the stage was set through Ham and his seed, who would loose an evil so great it would bring the judgment of fire.

Adam, the very first man, brought death into the world. His first son, Cain, and his ways, brought the flood, wiping out all of mankind except for eight. Finally, one of the eight, whom mankind had its fresh start through, was the source and seed that facilitated the third and final judgment of man. Let's review this in order to begin the judgment of fire.

The Woman Clothed with the Sun, and the Beast out of the Sea

NIV Rev 12:15 *Then from his mouth the serpent spewed water like a river, to overtake the woman and sweep her away with the torrent.*

NIV Rev 12:16 *But the earth helped the woman by opening its mouth and swallowing the river that the dragon had spewed out of his mouth.*

We must remember that Biblical prophecy has a way of combining the beginning and contemporary expression of the prophecy with the end and global expression. God, who gives these utterances to the prophets, sees both as one whole event, no matter how much time is entailed. He is outside of time. As such, it often becomes difficult to divide up what happens during the beginning and contemporary expression of what the prophecy speaks of, and what happens at the end of what the prophecy speaks of, meaning, the end of time (when it has had its total fulfillment). The key is to recognize that a prophecy applies to both beginning and end. Likewise, what was put into motion prophetically thousands of years ago may not have the final fulfillment for thousands of years to come. This is in spite of the fact that the contemporary manifestation may have had a seeming resolution or a finality to it in our own estimations, or according to our own perception. However, from God's estimation, the decreed prophecy is not complete until every single aspect of it is fulfilled according to His timing and purposes.

Through these verses, and logically so, we are to understand that this story starts with the new beginning of mankind after the flood. It starts with the eight people who survive the great flood and finally come to dry land.

The water the Devil spewed out is the flood. The earth opening up its mouth to swallow the waters to help the woman is the formations of the mountains, which rose above 12,000 feet (the height they were before the flood), in turn, created the ocean basins resulting in dry land again.

The next question is, who is this woman?

NIV Rev 12:1 *A great and wondrous sign appeared in heaven: a woman clothed with the sun, with the moon under her feet and a crown of twelve stars on her head.* *NIV Rev 12:2* *She was pregnant and cried out in pain as she was about to give birth.*

She represents not a single woman but a contingency of people. Going backwards, she is ultimately the bride of Christ (the Church, Jewish believers, and the 144,000). Going further back towards her origin, she and her lineage are the ones who gave birth to the Christ. She is the twelve tribes of Israel, the people of God whose father is Abraham, the father of faith. We know this because she wears a crown of twelve stars, which represent the twelve tribes of Israel. The woman and the bride consisting of many people and her origin through the Israelites, are one in the eyes of God. That is why He includes her origin (the Israelites) as the woman clothed with the sun.

However, just as the beast is the seed of one who was on the ark, Abraham also is the seed of one who was on the ark. Just as the beast was the seed of Ham who was the evil son of Noah, Abraham was the seed of

Shem, the righteous son of Noah. Abraham's seed is the seed from which the woman came (Ch 1:17-27). Consequently, the woman, whom the dragon hates, has her origins from the seed of Shem.

NIV Rev 12:17 Then the dragon was enraged at the woman and went off to make war against the rest of her offspring—those who obey God's commandments and hold to the testimony of Jesus.

NIV Rev 13:1 And the dragon stood on the shore of the sea. And I saw a beast coming out of the sea. He had ten horns and seven heads, with ten crowns on his horns, and on each head a blasphemous name.

The Devil waited on dry land for the ark to come out of the sea. He didn't have to wait long. Out of the waters of the flood (the sea) came the one he was waiting for, Ham, by whose seed and whose sins would come Nimrod, the beast. The origin of the beast and his legacy of evil empires, coupled with his return to the earth from the dead out from Hades on his way to the lake of fire, are one in the eyes of God—the beginning and the end of the matter.

NIV Rev 13:2 The beast I saw resembled a leopard, but had feet like those of a bear and a mouth like that of a lion. The dragon gave the beast his power and his throne and great authority.

These are the bodily forms and characteristics of the ensuing empires of the beast, just as the different metals of the statue of Nimrod in Nebuchadnezzar's dream represented the same empires.

NIV Rev 13:3 One of the heads of the beast seemed to have had a fatal wound, but the fatal wound had been healed. The whole world was astonished and followed the beast.

NIV Rev 13:4 Men worshiped the dragon because he had given authority to the beast, and they also worshiped the beast and asked, "Who is like the beast? Who can make war against him?"

This is the original head of the beast, the one who started it all, Nimrod, the founder of Babylon. The other heads are significant kings who started the different ensuing empires of Babylon, taking over from the previous one. For example, one of the heads is Alexander the Great, who was the king and founder of the Greek Empire (one of the empirical legacies of the beast).

Nimrod was killed by a head wound and will astonish the whole world when he comes back to life. He will be unkillable when he comes back. For it is the judgment of God that he, like all others who are doomed for destruction, must endure a second death by being thrown alive into the lake of fire. Because he will rise up from his first death (a fatal head wound), he can't be killed (so that the end which was decreed for him will come to pass). Ignorant of his real fate and the real reason he cannot be killed will result in many fearing him, seeing him as invincible, and, thus, futile to fight.

NIV Rev 13:5 The beast was given a mouth to utter proud words and blasphemies and to exercise his authority for forty-two months.
NIV Rev 13:6 He opened his mouth to blaspheme God, and to slander his name and his dwelling place and those who live in heaven.
NIV Rev 13:7 He was given power to make war against the saints and to conquer them. And he was given authority over every tribe, people, language and nation.

Nimrod fearlessly rails against God, who once killed all of the people of the earth with the flood. He proudly challenges God in a fight to the death in order to protect the people of the world from God's future judgments. Verse 5 is referring to Nimrod's return as the antichrist (the other savior).

When Nimrod returns, he continues to rail against God and proudly defies Him trying to goad Him into the ultimate battle. Verse 7 is very important; it says that God gave Nimrod the power to war against the saints and be triumphant over them. The saints are the offspring of the woman who was clothed with the sun, and also is the woman who rides the beast, the whore of Babylon. The woman who was clothed with the sun and her offspring that remain pure are the *Church Pure*, who will be raptured from the earth.

The offspring of the woman who was clothed with the sun, who became corrupt through empowering themselves with the spirit of Babylon, are the *Church Corrupt*. It has been decreed by God that the antichrist will have 42 months (3-1/2 years; 1,260 days) in which he will have free reign to destroy the *Church Corrupt* and the people who comprise her.

NIV Rev 17:16 *The beast and the ten horns you saw will hate the prostitute. They will bring her to ruin and leave her naked; they will eat her flesh and burn her with fire.*
NIV Rev 17:17 *For God has put it into their hearts to accomplish his purpose by agreeing to give the beast their power to rule, until God's words are fulfilled.*

NIV Da 12:7 *The man clothed in linen, who was above the waters of the river, lifted his right hand and his left hand toward heaven, and I heard him swear by him who lives forever, saying, "It will be for a time, times and half a time (3-1/2 years). When the power of the holy people has been finally broken, all these things will be completed.*

The *Church Corrupt*, who will go through this great tribulation, are also the darnel (weeds resembling wheat) that are gathered together from among the wheat at the harvest and are burned in the fire, which Jesus speaks of in His parable. This fire is the great tribulation and the destruction of Babylon (in the Church). The great tribulation is used by God as a means to purify the corrupt contingency of His Church, resulting in the great multitude that are given celestial bodies (clean white robes). Paul speaks of this:

NIV 1Co 3:10 ... *But each one should be careful how he builds.*

NIV 1Co 3:11 *For no one can lay any foundation other than the one already laid, which is Jesus Christ.*

NIV 1Co 3:12 *If any man builds on this foundation using gold, silver, costly stones, wood, hay or straw,*

NIV 1Co 3:13 *his work will be shown for what it is, because the Day will bring it to light. It will be revealed with fire, and the fire will test the quality of each man's work.*

NIV 1Co 3:14 *If what he has built survives, he will receive his reward.*

NIV 1Co 3:15 *If it is burned up, he will suffer loss; he himself will be saved, but only as one escaping through the flames.*

Revelation says of them:

NIV Rev 7:13 *Then one of the elders asked me, "These in white robes—who are they, and where did they come from?"*

NIV Rev 7:14 *I answered, "Sir, you know." And he said, "These are they who have come out of the great tribulation; they have washed their robes and made them white in the blood of the Lamb.*

NIV Rev 7:15 *Therefore, "they are before the throne of God and serve him day and night in his temple; and he who sits on the throne will spread his tent over them.*

NIV Rev 7:16 *Never again will they hunger; never again will they thirst. The sun will not beat upon them, nor any scorching heat.*

NIV Rev 7:17 *For the Lamb at the center of the throne will be their shepherd; he will lead them to springs of living water. And God will wipe away every tear from their eyes."*

The wheat that is gathered and brought to His barn is the *Church Pure*, who will be raptured from the earth and become celestial humans, avoiding the great tribulation.

NIV Rev 13:8 *All inhabitants of the earth will worship the beast—all whose names have not been written in the book of life belonging to the Lamb that was slain from the creation of the world.*

NIV Rev 13:9 *He who has an ear, let him hear.*

NIV Rev 13:10 *If anyone is to go into captivity, into captivity he will go. If anyone is to be killed with the sword, with the sword he will be killed.*

This calls for patient endurance and faithfulness on the part of the saints.

NIV Rev 17:8 *The beast, which you saw, once was, now is not, and will come up out of the Abyss and go to his destruction. The inhabitants of the earth whose names have not been written in the book of life from the creation of the world will be astonished when they see the beast, because he once was, now is not, and yet will come.*

The balance of the people in the world who are neither the *Church Pure* nor the *Church Corrupt,* the ones not written in the Lamb's book of life, will worship the beast. Those alive as well as those who are dead will be amazed at his return from the Abyss, as Revelation tells us. They all will rally behind him as their leader and king, their savior, who will (supposedly) protect them from the judgment of God.

However, for those Christians who are made clean and acceptable to God through the great tribulation, verse 10 gives the chilling reality of their unchangeable fate, "If anyone is to go into captivity, into captivity he will go. If anyone is to be killed with the sword, with the sword he will be killed." They are admonished to endure with faithfulness and patience, knowing there is a prize to be won, a celestial existence and life eternal.

We have shown the origins of the woman clothed with the sun to be the seed of Shem, the righteous son of Noah who came out of the flood (the sea). Likewise, we have shown the origin of the beast to be the seed of

Ham, the evil sinner, who came out of the flood. Now we will show the beginning of the outpouring of the judgment of fire:

The First Four of the Seven Seals

NIV Rev 6:1 *I watched as the Lamb opened the first of the seven seals. Then I heard one of the four living creatures say in a voice like thunder, "Come!"*
NIV Rev 6:2 *I looked, and there before me was a white horse! Its rider held a bow, and he was given a crown, and he rode out as a conqueror bent on conquest.*
NIV Rev 6:3 *When the Lamb opened the second seal, I heard the second living creature say, "Come!"*
NIV Rev 6:4 *Then another horse came out, a fiery red one. Its rider was given power to take peace from the earth and to make men slay each other. To him was given a large sword.*
NIV Rev 6:5 *When the Lamb opened the third seal, I heard the third living creature say, "Come!" I looked, and there before me was a black horse! Its rider was holding a pair of scales in his hand.*
NIV Rev 6:6 *Then I heard what sounded like a voice among the four living creatures, saying, "A quart of wheat for a day's wages, and three quarts of barley for a day's wages, and do not damage the oil and the wine!"*
NIV Rev 6:7 *When the Lamb opened the fourth seal, I heard the voice of the fourth living creature say, "Come!"*
NIV Rev 6:8 *I looked, and there before me was a pale horse! Its rider was named Death, and Hades was following close behind him. They were given power over a fourth of the earth to kill by sword, famine and plague, and by the wild beasts of the earth.*

The seven seals reveal the implementation of the judgment of fire. The first four seals are released simultaneously. The fifth is released by itself. The sixth and seventh are released simultaneously, like the first four.

Nimrod gathered the people to the cities he built, taking the example of the pre-flood Cain who had done the same thing. This was done in defiance of God, who admonished the people to spread out across the whole earth to settle and cultivate it. God wanted to avoid the evil that brought on the flood. Nimrod had decided that he could cultivate strength and power by bringing the people together into a confined location—a city. This was his first demonstration of dividing against God.

Note: Large urban centers, as much as they may seemingly be the greatest source of the good life for man, are the design of the Devil and the beast. It has been this way since Cain. People are more easily swayed, controlled, monitored, and enslaved in big cities. The opposite is true when the people are spread out over great distances, which is God's plan. It was the first phase of Nimrod's plan to fashion an empire by creating large urban areas or walled-in cities where he could influence, dominate, and enslave the people easier. This he did, and he was accredited for building many different great cities, some of which still exist today. However, he was not the father of the large urban center. That credit goes to Cain (Gen. 4:17), whose pre-flood wisdom Nimrod employed.

Secondly, within his city, Nimrod built a tower with the intention for it to rise up as high as the heavens and, thereby, protect him and his people if God should choose to destroy them once again in a flood. By this, he is again showing the progressive stance he is taking against God. In addition, (1) his hope was that the tower would be so high that he could climb it and go into the heavens to kill Yahweh. (2) The tower was used as a place to worship false gods and idols. These systems were invented by Nimrod so that, in his hatred and defiance against God, he could have something to offer the people that would cause them to divide from God and unite with him in his defiance.

In answer, God destroys the tower. He spreads the people throughout the earth, dividing them into 70 nations. In addition, he gives the 70 different nations 70 different languages, so that they can no longer speak a common language and thereby rally together as one people unified in defiance of God.

This is a radically miraculous and powerful intervention on God's part. Despite how devastatingly fearful God's response was, it was firm, resolute, decisive, kind, and disarming. This response by God did not, however, humble Nimrod, by any means. It filled him with more hatred and resolve to oppose God and protect himself and his people from God's power.

He went right back to work, picking up the pieces and establishing his kingdom. Next, out of defiance of God's solution, Nimrod gathered an army and defeated the nation next to him, Assyria. This is why he is also known as, "the Assyrian." He started by taking one of the other 69 nations and making it his own. When the people saw his courage, strength, and bold defiance against the commands of God, they put themselves under him and made him the king of all the people of the earth. With Nimrod as their protector and leader, they felt that they too could do as they willed and not suffer the judgments of God.

When God saw the stark rebellion and defiance of Nimrod against Him coupled with the people of the earth crowning Nimrod king over them and unanimously joining in defiance against Him, He pronounced the final judgment of fire against the whole earth and the people in it. He began by releasing the first four of the sealed decrees of the judgment of fire.

Life on the earth changed suddenly just as it had when everyone was spread around the world and given 70 different nations with 70 different languages. The earth became a hostile place to live. Sickness, natural disasters, famine, deadly hostility from nature against man from the wild beast, and even war were introduced into the world. Just like when Adam and Eve's eyes were opened and they had to face God, realizing the gravity of what they had done, so did the entire world have to do when these things came about.

According to the Bible, God later refers to these deadly, life-taking curses as His four winds (of destruction)0. They were almost exclusively called upon to bring judgment against peoples and nations whose rebellions and abominations had piled high into the heavens.

This is a most important point to take in if you are to understand the world through the story of Christianity. The four winds of destruction bring people down to Hades, where they are collected and imprisoned, disembodied, awaiting the resurrection of the dead when they will be resurrected (once again clothed with a body) and judged according to their deeds.

The four horses and riders, are the first four seals. The horses represent the different powers God has granted, and the riders are celestial beings who direct the power of the horses by the reins in their hands and bit and bridle in the horses' mouths. These powers and their riders were granted to the Devil, who in turn, granted it to his human agent, the beast, and whoever else he sees fit to empower.

In the Bible, it talks about the attempted seduction of Jesus at the end of His 40 day fast. At this time, the Devil took Jesus to a high place and showed Him all of the cities of the world. These cities were the different cities of Babylon. He offered them all to Jesus if He would just bow down to him. What he offered Jesus was under his authority and was his to offer. However, the Devil had already granted this authority over the great cities of the earth to the beast, Nimrod. Being true to his nature, he was prepared to take them away from Nimrod and give them to Jesus, without the slightest qualm of integrity disturbing him. What he offered Jesus was indeed a real temptation of substance.

An important thing to recognize is something that will answer an age old question that comes up in every human heart who searches for an answer. That question is: "Why is there war and starvation and sickness in the world?" This question creates a burden in the human heart of those who care to find cures for diseases, trying to eradicate sickness forever. Likewise, it burdens those who fight against injustice, enslavement, and war, trying to eradicate man's hostility against man. It also motivates people to find ways to overcome the famines and natural disasters in the world, putting an end to starvation. Although these noble quests are important for us to participate in, showing that we care about our fellow man, they are unwinnable battles. No one seems to realize that we are under the curses of the judgment of fire and that these are simply preludes to the death that will swallow up the entire natural universe when the time comes.

The four winds of destruction are powers (which have been granted by God) to take away the lives of an ongoing 25% of the world's population. No dreams, aspirations, powers, or will of man can change this until the white horse and its rider—Jesus, whose robe has been dipped in blood— come to rule the earth and all of the earth's nations for 1,000 years. He alone will have a power great enough to destroy the power of the four horsemen.

We know this to be true because when He was here, Jesus showed that He indeed had a greater power than the four horsemen. He revealed it when He cast out every demon, cured the sick, healed the wounds, and rose people from the dead. In addition, He rebuked the storms, walked on the water, and miraculously fed multitudes. In doing so, He demonstrated that His power was above that of the four horsemen, and above that of any mortal man.

The fact that historically He did these things assures us and makes it easy to believe that when Jesus returns He will have the power to completely eradicate the power of the four horsemen. He will even make it so that wild beasts and venomous snakes will no longer be violent, nor will they harm humans. Also humans will not have the power, charisma, and strength to unite people together to war, conquer, and enslave. In fact, large urban centers and industrial conglomerates will not exist in God's Kingdom. Such a thing requires leave from God, as well as power from God, to do so. As John the Baptist said:

KJV Jn 3:27 ... *man can receive nothing, except it be given him from heaven.*

Until the return of Jesus, whenever advancements cure deadly illness and decrease the amount of people who die by illness, the lack of mortality will be made up for by famines in the world, wars, and natural disasters. Eliminate famines and distribute the world food supply so no one dies of starvation, then wars, illness, and natural disasters will claim the deficit of human lives created by the noble efforts to end world hunger. God has granted that an ongoing 25% of the people in the world, generation after generation, will meet a premature end to their lives by his four winds of destruction.

This is the curse we live under. The ground became a curse to Adam for bringing death into the world. This curse caused it to produce thorns and thistles for him. This meant that all of the types of foods that man needed to survive no longer naturally grew in abundance without any efforts. Instead, thorns, thistles, and weeds began to naturally grow from the earth in abundance. As a result, it was by the exhausting struggles of Adam's hard labor and by the sweat of his brow that the ground would finally produce food for him and his family to survive. It has been that way ever since for all of mankind. Although it is a labor of love and good, honest, hard work to grow things from the ground, nevertheless, it is a curse on mankind that we have to do so.

Likewise, since the rebellion of Nimrod, we have struggled to survive, almost hopelessly, under the curses that were released because of his rebellion and the willingness of the people of the earth to put themselves under him in defiance of God.

Again, it is hopeless to fight these curses, however, it is the struggle and burden of man to do everything he can in order to survive in the midst of them. From a bird's eye view, these curses are the product of man wanting to enslave his fellow man and empower himself in an effort to selfishly serve himself. Yet, in God granting these powers to the evil men who hunger and thirst for them, it is clear that these calamities force out into the open a necessity and drive for man to serve something other than himself out of his concern for his brother human beings.

This idea is supported by what Abraham was told by God when He was blessing him. Before his seed had a chance to do anything wrong, God told Abraham that his descendents would have to serve as slaves for 400 years. On the surface, it seems odd that in blessing someone with children so abundant that they become a nation, He would at the same time doom them with 400 years of harsh and cruel slavery.

The truth is, God doesn't wave a magic wand and reprogram the hearts of people as He would reprogram software for a computer. Otherwise, people would be for Him like dolls who say whatever He wants them to say when He pulls the string on their backs.

No, He gives people free will. However, possessing the knowledge of good and evil has poisoned people's hearts to the degree that they see themselves as divided from God, and they see themselves as the center of the world. Therefore, their perception is that they must serve self instead of God. In order to make a people for Himself, God must change people's hearts so that they are different from the rest of man. They must learn how to serve God and not self. This is the hardest thing for God to overcome inside of people's hearts. Since wisdom of the spirit really is experiential knowledge, it takes real life experiences to change the heart and outlook of a man. As such, extreme experiences are required to change the natural, inborn, sinful outlook, that gives man his perception of life (to serve self).

God knew exactly what it would take to turn the hearts of men; He wanted Abraham's descendants to be a people who loved Him and served Him like Abraham their father. To just leave Abraham's children to their own devises would be to doom them into never breaking free from the outlook of serving self. This was proven through the children of Noah, the righteous man, whose offspring brought back the evils of the pre-flood world.

Although harsh and cruel, decreeing that they should be enslaved under forced servitude for 400 years is what God deemed would experientially change their hearts. He thereby allowed them to be enslaved, and tempered them, so that they would learn to serve something other than self. He made sure that they would become a people who would experientially, even forcefully, be disciplined into forming within themselves the capacity to serve God by their experience under forced servitude, and thereby change their outlook.

The question will always remain, or it will always be about the decision in each human heart to either serve self or serve God. To serve self will put you under the authority of the Devil, his antichrist, and their power of the four horsemen. To serve God will take you out from underneath that power and put you under the One who rides the white horse, with His robe dipped in blood and on His thigh written, "KING OF KINGS AND LORD OF LORDS". He will bring the person who decides to serve God out from under the four winds of destruction and into the bliss of His eternal Kingdom.

Again, at the end of the day, the choice is this: Serve self and be under the power of the Devil, his antichrist, and their power of the four horsemen, or serve God and be plucked out from underneath that power to live in eternal bliss.

These extreme conditions really are necessary in order to cultivate unselfishness and servitude in man's heart. They will, thereby, create the necessary hearts that will make them fit to become celestial humans and live for eternity. This alone will allow God to keep His promise to Noah that He will not destroy all of the people of the world ever again.

As a part of the release of the four horsemen and granting Nimrod to be king over the people of the earth as they desired, God was also setting the stage and the way for salvation to come. The first order of business was to do something to begin a change of outlook in the hearts of the objects of His mercy. He gives the objects of His wrath what they wish, as short lived as it is, to use as a means to purify with fire the recipients of His mercy. All who are saved must endure their own personal tribulations to make their hearts right.

The next step in His plan, the fifth seal, brings mercy to the condemned people of the earth and a way out from under our death sentence.

The Fifth Seal

NIV Rev 6:9 *When he opened the fifth seal, I saw under the altar the souls of those who had been slain because of the word of God and the testimony they had maintained.*

NIV Rev 6:10 *They called out in a loud voice, "How long, Sovereign Lord, holy and true, until you judge the inhabitants of the earth and avenge our blood?"*

NIV Rev 6:11 *Then each of them was given a white robe, and they were told to wait a little longer, until the number of their fellow servants and brothers who were to be killed as they had been was completed.*

The release of this sealed decree of God's is actually the redeeming work that Jesus did on the cross by sacrificing His life. It could be said that the reason these disembodied souls under the altar cried out looking for justice against those who would kill the people of God is because they had enough when Jesus, the King of Glory, was also martyred and then counted among them.

One of the things that gives us evidence that Jesus' sacrificial death was the fifth seal is that, in addition to the souls suddenly looking for justice, they were given clean white robes. For a soul (which is a disembodied person) to be given a white robe means being given a celestial body. If it really was a fabric robe, it would be a cruel joke, because disembodied souls have no body by which to wear a robe with. This would be like offering an expensive pair of shoes to a person who had both of his legs amputated. There are two occasions in Revelation where people are referred to as "souls." In both occasions, this being one of them, they were talking about dead people. They are referred to as "souls" because they do not have a body. They do not have a body because they are dead.

When it says that these disembodied souls were given white robes, they were granted a celestial body to clothe their soul with. For this to have happened, Jesus had to have finished His redeeming work on the cross, Otherwise, no one would be able to become a celestial human with a celestial body until after the last day.

NIV Mt 27:50 *And when Jesus had cried out again in a loud voice, he gave up his spirit.*
NIV Mt 27:51 *At that moment the curtain of the temple was torn in two from top to bottom. The earth shook and the rocks split.*

NIV Mt 27:52 The tombs broke open and the bodies of many holy people who had died were raised to life.

NIV Mt 27:53 They came out of the tombs, and after Jesus' resurrection they went into the holy city and appeared to many people.

NIV Mt 27:54 When the centurion and those with him who were guarding Jesus saw the earthquake and all that had happened, they were terrified, and exclaimed, "Surely he was the Son of God!"

It says that Jesus was given the keys to Hades, the gates of hell could not prevail against Him, and that He set the prisoners free. While in the grave for 3 days, Jesus went to Hades and set free from it the first group of people. They are identified as the 144,000. They are the first fruits of Jesus' redeeming work. They were the first to rise from the dead, receive a celestial body and be able to have direct fellowship with both the Father and the Son. These 144,000 are part of the people who comprise the woman clothed with the sun. They were the ones who kept both their hearts and their DNA pure. It was also through their lineage of DNA that Jesus was born when He took on the form of a mortal man. This is why they are so special in His eyes.

The Lamb and the 144,000

NIV Rev 14:1 Then I looked, and there before me was the Lamb, standing on Mount Zion, and with him 144,000 who had his name and his Father's name written on their foreheads.

The reason the "Lamb" is standing on Mount Zion is because it is there that He did His redeeming work through His own sacrificial death. Thus, He is called the Lamb and, as such, He has been raised from the dead. With Him are those that He set free, the first fruits to benefit from His redeeming work. It is promised that wherever He is, they will be with Him (just like it is spoken of all who are declared His bride). Verse 4 below says that they were purchased from among men; Jesus had paid the price with His life and the 144,000 were the first to cash in—the first fruits.

NIV Rev 14:2 And I heard a sound from heaven like the roar of rushing waters and like a loud peal of thunder. The sound I heard was like that of harpists playing their harps.

NIV Rev 14:3 And they sang a new song before the throne and before the four living creatures and the elders. No one could learn the song except the 144,000 who had been redeemed from the earth.

NIV Rev 14:4 These are those who did not defile themselves with women, for they kept themselves pure. They follow the Lamb wherever he goes. They were purchased from among men and offered as firstfruits to God and the Lamb.

Even though they were held captive in a paradisiacal place of Hades (under the altar), they were still, nevertheless, disembodied souls unable to have direct fellowship with God until Jesus rescued them from that place. Because of His sacrifice, these 144,000 were given a body by which to fellowship with God. We see the proof of this in the Gospel of Matthew. When Jesus' redeeming work was finished at the cross, this 144,000—the first fruits—rose from the dead and spoke to the people in the city of Jerusalem.

Mt 27:50 And when Jesus had cried out again in a loud voice, he gave up his spirit.

Mt 27:51 At that moment the curtain of the temple was torn in two from top to bottom. The earth shook and the rocks split.

Mt 27:52 The tombs broke open and the bodies of many holy people who had died were raised to life.

Mt 27:53 They came out of the tombs, and after Jesus' resurrection they went into the holy city and appeared to many people.

When Jesus was finally able to lead the procession of these first fruits whom His work had produced to the Father, it was the most amazing accomplishment that had ever taken place! People of the earth who were given over to death and eternal separation from God now had a way to reconcile and come into direct fellowship with their God. It became true that Jesus is the way, the truth, and the life!

Note: These 144,000 have the prestige of being the "first fruits." What an amazing group to be one of! However, we, those born after Jesus' redeeming work up until the great tribulation, are part of a greater group than they. The 144,000 potentially could have spent more than an additional 1,000 years disembodied in the paradisiacal place of Hades. Many of them were dead for a long time. We, however, are promised that if we do His will, we will never experience death or have to face judgment. We have the potential to become celestial humans and receive our celestial bodies without tasting death. We have it the best, because this was not the case for the 144,000. Again, they had to die and become disembodied until Christ did His redeeming work, and it was only then that they could become celestial humans possessing celestial bodies.

As for the justice of their martyrdom, they must wait until God finishes using the evil in the earth to cleanse His people and make them fit for His Kingdom. Then, after that is accomplished, God will pour out His wrath and judgment on their enemies, giving the perfect justice to those whose blood was spilled. The time when this happens is called the time of wrath, which immediately follows the great tribulation.

From then on (after the 144,000), all those who embody Jesus' disembodied Spirit, will go from life to life. They will go from being a mortal human to becoming a celestial human, even before their heads hit the ground in death. This will last until shortly after the last seven, when all of the mortal men who embody His Spirit will be raised up to heaven (by His Spirit) and given a celestial body at the rapture.

After that, all who die to the body will once again go to Hades disembodied, whether they are His people (the saints) or not. Everyone after the rapture will go to Hades and await the last day when they will be resurrected and once again be embodied, or clothed, in order to face judgment. The only exception to this is those who participate in the first resurrection. The first resurrection is exclusively for those who die in the great tribulation while holding fast to their testimony and do not take the mark of the beast or worship his image—at the cost of their lives. They, too, will go to Hades, disembodied, when their body dies. However, in the days right before the seventh trumpet sounds they will arise from among the dead and become embodied with a celestial body to rule in God's Kingdom for 1,000 years with Jesus.

The sixth and seventh seals are opened simultaneously just as the first four were:

NIV Rev 6:12 I watched as he opened the sixth seal. There was a great earthquake. The sun turned black like sackcloth made of goat hair, the whole moon turned blood red,

NIV Rev 6:13 and the stars in the sky fell to earth, as late figs drop from a fig tree when shaken by a strong wind.

This is describing the time of the abomination that causes desolation spoken of in Daniel. It is after the second beast goes into the temple and sets up an image of Nimrod (the first beast), having put an end to the sacrifices made to God 3-1/2 years earlier. Then, through his abominable practices of magic and worship, either out of the image or the image itself comes alive, and Nimrod is loosed out of the Abyss. He was called to return from the dead with the purpose of saving the people of the world from the judgment of God as the antichrist (the other savior). The truth is that he is on his way to his second death of being thrown alive in the lake of fire after the battle of Armageddon.

The first thing Nimrod does is leave the temple and kill the two witnesses. Not only is he a giant, but he has come out from among the dead and is able to kill those whom no one can kill. Previously, any attempts by any humans to kill the two witnesses were met by the witnesses calling down fire and destroying them. So this act by the beast is a great wonder and a source of astonishment to the people of the world. It causes the people of the earth to celebrate that they are finally through with these two witnesses who caused a worldwide drought and performed many wondrous signs that distressed the people in order to get their attention. The Bible tells us that they will be so glad to be free of these two that they will celebrate and exchange gifts. It goes without saying that they will worship the beast all the more, chanting things like, "Who could ever challenge him? He is more powerful than them all!"

^{Amp Rev 13:4} . . . *they also praised and worshiped the beast, exclaiming, Who is a match for the beast, and, Who can make war against him?*

However, the two witnesses, after being left dead in the streets for 3-1/2 days, are called to their feet again and made alive. This horrifies the entire world! They are afraid that they are now in big trouble with these two witnesses. However, a voice calls from the heavens, instructing them to come up because they have accomplished their work. They were told to prophesy, giving witness for 1,260 days. They accomplished prophesying these amount of days when the beast appeared in the temple and then killed them.

This is not all that happens. In addition to them being called up to heaven, the Holy Spirit who had remained in the world, embodied in those who are in spiritual union with the Lord, also departs from the world, leaving it to itself. When He does so, He brings with Him all who are in spiritual union with the Him. This is in keeping to what Jesus promised at the last supper:

(1) He would come back to the world in His disembodied form of Spirit.

(2) He would be embodied within those who love Him by obeying Him.

(3) He would not leave them as orphans, but be with them and in them forever.

It is because of this promise and when His Holy Spirit withdraws from the world, creating a global desolation (an absence of God's Spirit in the world) due to the abomination, that He must take up with Him all who truly embodied His disembodied Spirit in the world. Otherwise, Jesus would be made a liar, deserting those who embodied His Spirit.

So when it says that there was a great earthquake in verse 12, it is talking about the moment that God will leave the world to the antichrist who came out of the Abyss and appeared in what was formerly God's holy temple. It is the moment that the two witnesses, those who share a New Covenant relationship with Jesus, and the Holy Spirit will all depart from the world. This begins the time of darkness that Jesus spoke about when nobody can do the work of the Father.

This is what is meant when it was said that the sun turned black like sackcloth: spiritual darkness took over. When it says that the stars fell to the earth like overripened figs from a fig tree under a strong wind, it is referring to the time of the great tribulation, when all who cling to their testimony of Jesus will be killed by the beast for not worshiping him or taking his mark.

NIV Rev 6:13 and the stars in the sky fell to earth, as late figs drop from a fig tree when shaken by a strong wind.

We already explained that when "the sun turned black like sackcloth," it is referring to the time of spiritual darkness that Jesus spoke of, a time when darkness will rule the earth. When it says the stars fell to earth . . . it is talking about the saints who are martyred. Their stature is like the stars in the heavens. When they are killed, they are the stars which fall to the earth. Daniel affirms this analogy:

NIV Da 12:3 Those who are wise will shine like the brightness of the heavens, and those who lead many to righteousness, like the stars for ever and ever.

It goes on to say: *as late figs drop from a fig tree when shaken by a strong wind.* This is a very carefully worded comparison by the One, Jesus, who cursed the fig tree. The late figs are the elect left behind during the great tribulation, that is why they are characterized as "late" figs. Them dropping from the tree is the elect being killed. The tree is the Church. The strong wind which shakes the tree is "the four winds of destruction" which are released without restraint because of the withdrawal of the Holy Spirit from the earth. Let's look at what Jesus says about fig trees.

Jesus Clears the Temple

NIV Mk 11:12 The next day as they were leaving Bethany, Jesus was hungry.
NIV Mk 11:13 Seeing in the distance a fig tree in leaf, he went to find out if it had any fruit. When he reached it, he found nothing but leaves, because it was not the season for figs.
NIV Mk 11:14 Then he said to the tree, "May no one ever eat fruit from you again."
And his disciples heard him say it.

It might seem over the top for Jesus to curse this fig tree just because it didn't bear fruit. However, Jesus was trying to make a point. Seeing the fig tree "in leaf" means it has the signs of having bore ripened fruit. This is to be compared with the Church approaching the last seven. It has all of the signs of being mature and ripe from a distance, however, at a closer inspection, it is bearing no fruit.

For this reason, Jesus spits the Church out of His mouth and curses her, condemning her forever, so that no one will ever eat of her fruit again. After the outpouring of the sixth seal, the Church's power, influence, and wealth will be stripped of her, even her people killed. She will be destroyed so thoroughly that never again will she rise up and be of influence. All of heaven will cheer when the smoke of her burning goes up to eternities of eternities (the lake of fire). This is how dimly Jesus views the modern Church and its leadership. It is an idea that we must not be astonished to hear or to learn of but, for the sake of our immortal souls, we must come to terms with. As for the people (saints) who suffer and die when this is carried out, Paul talks of them below:

NIV 1Co 3:10 *By the grace God has given me, I laid a foundation as an expert builder, and someone else is building on it. But each one should be careful how he builds.*

NIV 1Co 3:11 *For no one can lay any foundation other than the one already laid, which is Jesus Christ.*

NIV 1Co 3:12 *If any man builds on this foundation using gold, silver, costly stones, wood, hay or straw,*

NIV 1Co 3:13 *his work will be shown for what it is, because the Day will bring it to light. It will be revealed with fire, and the fire will test the quality of each man's work.*

NIV 1Co 3:14 *If what he has built survives, he will receive his reward.*

NIV 1Co 3:15 *If it is burned up, he will suffer loss; he himself will be saved, but only as one escaping through the flames.*

NIV 1Co 3:16 *Don't you know that you yourselves are God's temple and that God's Spirit lives in you?*

NIV 1Co 3:17 *If anyone destroys God's temple, God will destroy him; for God's temple is sacred, and you are that temple.*

NIV 1Co 3:18 *Do not deceive yourselves. If any one of you thinks he is wise by the standards of this age, he should become a "fool" so that he may become wise.*

NIV 1Co 3:19 *For the wisdom of this world is foolishness in God's sight. As it is written: "He catches the wise in their craftiness";*

NIV 1Co 3:20 *and again, "The Lord knows that the thoughts of the wise are futile."*

The day that will bring it to light and have it tested with fire is the day that the great tribulation will come. That fire of testing is the great tribulation. If what you build survives (constructed with your life's work), you will receive your reward. Your reward is this: to be taken up in the rapture and for your work to survive. If you are left behind and your life is destroyed, even to death, it says you will be saved but only as one escaping through the flames (without your works, which will burn in the fire). These are the people who hold fast to their testimony and do not worship the beast and do not accept his mark, even at the expense of their own lives.

As a result, you must go through these flames, which will test and consume everything in your life. You will suffer great loss, however, because of the faithfulness of your testimony, you (your soul) will survive. You will rise up from the dead at the first resurrection, and, along with those who live through it, be raised up above the earth joining Jesus in the sky, now possessing a celestial body. These combined people will be the great multitude beyond counting who, with clean white robes, will worship and thank Jesus for how He was able to salvage them.

After cursing the fig tree so that it would never bear fruit for anyone to partake of again, Jesus goes to the temple. By what He witnesses at the temple, we can see why He cursed the fig tree in this manner: as a warning to the Church.

NIV Mk 11:15 On reaching Jerusalem, Jesus entered the temple area and began driving out those who were buying and selling there. He overturned the tables of the money changers and the benches of those selling doves,
NIV Mk 11:16 and would not allow anyone to carry merchandise through the temple courts.
NIV Mk 11:17 And as he taught them, he said, "Is it not written: " 'My house will be called a house of prayer for all nations'?
But you have made it 'a den of robbers.'"

NIV Mk 11:18 *The chief priests and the teachers of the law heard this and began looking for a way to kill him, for they feared him, because the whole crowd was amazed at his teaching.*

NIV Mk 11:19 *When evening came, they went out of the city.*

NIV Mk 11:20 *In the morning, as they went along, they saw the fig tree withered from the roots.*

NIV Mk 11:21 *Peter remembered and said to Jesus, "Rabbi, look! The fig tree you cursed has withered!"*

We must take our lesson from the fig tree! Jesus' mercy only goes so far. This curse on the Church is Jesus vomiting her out of His mouth. It also is the reason that He admonishes us to "come out of her, my people."

NIV Rev 18:4 *Then I heard another voice from heaven say: "Come out of her, my people, so that you will not share in her* (the *Church Corrupt) sins, so that you will not receive any of her plagues;*

NIV Rev 18:5 *for her sins are piled up to heaven, and God has remembered her crimes.*

And again, Jesus compares the Church with the fig tree:

Repent or Perish

NIV Lk 13:1 *Now there were some present at that time who told Jesus about the Galileans whose blood Pilate had mixed with their sacrifices.*

NIV Lk 13:2 *Jesus answered, "Do you think that these Galileans were worse sinners than all the other Galileans because they suffered this way?*

NIV Lk 13:3 *I tell you, no! But unless you repent, you too will all perish.*

NIV Lk 13:4 *Or those eighteen who died when the tower in Siloam fell on them—do you think they were more guilty than all the others living in Jerusalem?*

NIV Lk 13:5 *I tell you, no! But unless you repent, you too will all perish."*

NIV Lk 13:6 *Then he told this parable: "A man had a fig tree, planted in his vineyard, and he went to look for fruit on it, but did not find any.*

NIV Lk 13:7 So he said to the man who took care of the vineyard, 'For three years now I've been coming to look for fruit on this fig tree and haven't found any. Cut it down! Why should it use up the soil?'

NIV Lk 13:8 " 'Sir,' the man replied, 'leave it alone for one more year, and I'll dig around it and fertilize it.

NIV Lk 13:9 If it bears fruit next year, fine! If not, then cut it down.' "

Verses 8-9 reflect the genuine patience and longsuffering of the Lord. He gives us all of the time and space we could possibly need and every opportunity to bear fruit for Him by being the temple of His Holy Spirit.

NIV 2Pe 3:9 The Lord is not slow in keeping his promise, as some understand slowness. He is patient with you, not wanting anyone to perish, but everyone to come to repentance.

NIV 2Pe 3:10 But the day of the Lord will come like a thief. The heavens will disappear with a roar; the elements will be destroyed by fire, and the earth and everything in it will be laid bare.

NIV 2Pe 3:11 Since everything will be destroyed in this way, what kind of people ought you to be? You ought to live holy and godly lives

NIV 2Pe 3:12 as you look forward to the day of God and speed its coming. That day will bring about the destruction of the heavens by fire, and the elements will melt in the heat.

NIV 2Pe 3:13 But in keeping with his promise we are looking forward to a new heaven and a new earth, the home of righteousness.

To bear fruit means to allow His Spirit to have expression through our lives so that it is no longer us that live, meaning we no longer live a life of our own choosing. Instead, we live to carry out every prompting of the Spirit, and thus give Him our spiritual worship and become in New Covenant relationship with Him.

There is no doubt that when the sixth seal tells us that the stars fall to the earth like late figs fall to the ground when shaken by a strong wind, it is talking about the 3-1/2 years of the great tribulation and the deaths of all of the saints that will happen during that time period. Amen.

Next, as a part of the sixth seal:

NIV Rev 6:14 The sky receded like a scroll, rolling up, and every mountain and island was removed from its place.

NIV Rev 6:15 Then the kings of the earth, the princes, the generals, the rich, the mighty, and every slave and every free man hid in caves and among the rocks of the mountains.

NIV Rev 6:16 They called to the mountains and the rocks, "Fall on us and hide us from the face of him who sits on the throne and from the wrath of the Lamb!

NIV Rev 6:17 For the great day of their wrath has come, and who can stand?"

Verses 14-17 speak of the end of the 1,260 days of great tribulation endured by the saints of God. Immediately afterwards, the wrath of God begins. It is then poured out on the world, avenging the martyred and satisfying the prayers of those under the altar. It is punishment poured out on Nimrod, the other savior, and his kingdom of followers.

The tables have turned and the saints who have survived the great tribulation now have a mark on their forehead from God that won't allow them to be killed by the antichrist or be effected by the plagues that befall the kingdom of the antichrist. This is just as the Israelites were not affected by the plagues that befell the Egyptians who enslaved them. It also means this: that the Holy Spirit and the agents of heaven are active in the earth again after a half an hour of silence/inactivity (3-1/2 years).

Here is a literal phenomena that will occur. It says that the sky will open up like a scroll and the people of the earth will now be able to see directly into heaven 8 out of every 24 hours a day. It is a literal tearing of the fabric of space and time that the earth will eventually be pushed through when it departs the natural universe with its atmosphere. It will then reside in the spirit realm. It doesn't move geographically, however, it moves from one dimension into another.

NIV Rev 8:12 *The fourth angel sounded his trumpet, and a third of the sun was struck, a third of the moon, and a third of the stars, so that a third of them turned dark. A third of the day was without light, and also a third of the night.*

Verse 12 tells us more about the sky rolling up like a scroll or this tear in the fabric of space and time. As the earth rotates, it has 12 hours of daylight when the sun comes out, then 12 hours of night sky when the moon and the stars come out. However, somewhere between the two, 4 hours (1/3) of the day sky with the sun are taken away. Likewise, 4 hours (1/3) of the night sky with the moon and the stars are no more. This leaves 8 hours each for the day sky and the night sky instead of the normal 12 hours. Thereby leaving 1/3 of every 24 hour day (which is 8 hours), as a view of the spirit realm that allows one to see, when looking up in the sky, the Lord poised to come down and conquer the world.

Again, at this event during the 24 hours rotation of the earth, the sky from horizon to horizon will show:

(1) the day sky with the sun for 8 hours; then followed by

(2) an opening in the sky which reveals the spirit realm from horizon to horizon for 8 hours; then finally

(3) for the last 8 hours of its rotation, it will show in the sky from horizon to horizon the night sky with the stars and the moon.

This phenomena does not just happen like something magical, but it is a violent tearing of the fabric of space and time. It said that there will be an earthquake so violent that it will rearrange the whole topography of the entire earth, possibly bringing it back to its pre-flood conditions. The mountains will be removed and lowered, the ocean floors raised up, and the continents pushed back together, taking away the islands.

We learn later that the entire earth will be pushed out of the natural universe all the way through this tear in space, like a baby is pushed by the labor of birth through the cervix of a woman and comes out into the world. The entire earth eventually leaves the natural universe, with its atmosphere, and is pushed fully into the spirit realm. This means that there is no sun to bring light to the day sky and there are no stars, and moon to bring light from the night sky. If the earth continues to rotate, it will be 24 hours of the same sky, darkness, because there are no stars and it is no longer part of a solar system. This is verified when it says that the kingdom of the beast is plunged into total darkness.

NIV Rev 16:10 *The fifth angel poured out his bowl on the throne of the beast, and his kingdom was plunged into darkness. Men gnawed their tongues in agony* *NIV Rev 16:11* *and cursed the God of heaven . . .*

These above verses are fulfilled when the earth is totally pushed into the dimension of the spirit realm and out of the natural universe. This is supported by the fact that, after this, many of the evil celestial beings and much of what was imprisoned in Hades is let loose in the earth. Man then suffers from these supernatural creatures during these days of wrath against the world.

It stands to reason that the purpose of the earth moving into the spirit realm is so that the spiritual and the natural can interact with each other and be visible to each other. It is under this condition that the inhabitants of the celestial city, the New Jerusalem, are able to interact, minister to, and rule the mortals on the earth. It also becomes the time when it says that there is no need for the sun and the stars and the moon because the light that spills out of the New Jerusalem illuminates the whole world.

NIV Rev 21:23 *The city does not need the sun or the moon to shine on it, for the glory of God gives it light, and the Lamb is its lamp.*
NIV Rev 21:24 *The nations will walk by its light, and the kings of the earth will bring their splendor into it.*
NIV Rev 21:25 *On no day will its gates ever be shut, for there will be no night there.*

However, we are getting a little bit ahead. Before the condition that is described in verses 21:23-25 comes, there will be many things that the people of the earth will suffer from first.

The Seventh Seal:

NIV Rev 8:1 *When he opened the seventh seal, there was silence in heaven for about half an hour.*

The seventh seal was opened simultaneously with the sixth. We know this because it starts out by saying that when the seventh seal was opened, there was silence in heaven for about a half an hour. A half an hour is metaphoric for a half of a cycle, meaning half of a 7 year time period, or for 3-1/2 years. That time period is the silence or inactivity of heaven during the global desolation of the great tribulation. The sixth seal activity began with the great tribulation. The seventh seal was opened at the same time but has to wait until the great tribulation finishes before it can begin its activity of the outpouring of God's wrath.

Both seals have to do with the pouring out of God's judgment. The sixth seal is focused, however, on the judgment of His saints. It is the last resort that God must take to purify those He loves so that they may become the great multitude and have a share in His Kingdom as the bride of His Son during His reign on earth over the mortals.

NIV 1Pe 4:12 Dear friends, do not be surprised at the painful trial you are suffering, as though something strange were happening to you.

NIV 1Pe 4:13 But rejoice that you participate in the sufferings of Christ, so that you may be overjoyed when his glory is revealed.

NIV 1Pe 4:14 If you are insulted because of the name of Christ, you are blessed, for the Spirit of glory and of God rests on you.

NIV 1Pe 4:15 If you suffer, it should not be as a murderer or thief or any other kind of criminal, or even as a meddler.

NIV 1Pe 4:16 However, if you suffer as a Christian, do not be ashamed, but praise God that you bear that name.

NIV 1Pe 4:17 For it is time for judgment to begin with the family of God; and if it begins with us, what will the outcome be for those who do not obey the gospel of God?

NIV Pe 4:18 And, "If it is hard for the righteous to be saved, what will become of the ungodly and the sinner?"

NIV 1Pe 4:19 So then, those who suffer according to God's will should commit themselves to their faithful Creator and continue to do good.

The seventh seal, just as the sixth, is about the outpouring of God's judgment. However, it has more to do with the outpouring of God's wrath, meaning His punishment against the world for the injustices they have committed against His people. This will bring all prophecy, concerning the eradication of evil in the earth, to a close. Both are opened simultaneously, because both are the outpouring of His judgment. The sixth is focused on the discipline of the saints. The seventh must wait until the sixth is finished and the full number of saints are harvested. Then, the seventh will be unleashed on the world, who are the true objects of His wrath.

NIV 1Pe 4:17 *For it is time for judgment to begin with the family of God; and if it begins with us, what will the outcome be for those who do not obey the gospel of God?*

The Bible tells us that the second beast (who is the false prophet and prepares the way for the beast/antichrist) kicks off the final seven when he makes treaties with many nations. The two witnesses basically come after the halfway point of that last seven, when the false prophet ceases the sacrifices in the temple. We are told that the two witnesses prophesy to the world of God's coming wrath for 1,260 days (3-1/2 years). They do this with a backdrop of the work that the second beast does to prepare the way for the antichrist (the other savior).

Exactly 1,290 days after he prohibits the sacrifices in the temple, we are told that the false prophet sets up an image of the beast in the temple. This happens after the completion of the last seven, marking the end of the 70-7's decreed by God. Within the next 45 days, several things happen. At the high point of the false prophet's worship of the first beast, the antichrist comes up out of the grave through the image, or the image itself somehow comes to life. The beast finally has come back from the grave to have his day.

His first act is to kill the two witnesses and begin the persecution of the saints. However, within those 45 days and 3-1/2 days after (1) the beast comes alive, (2) the two witnesses are killed, then they rise back to life. They will terrify the whole world in doing so. Then exactly 1,335 days after the sacrifices had ended (45 days after the image of the beast was set up), the Holy Spirit will withdraw from the earth, creating a global desolation, and those who are in a New Covenant relationship with Jesus will be raptured along with the two witnesses.

Refer to Last Seven Timeline at the end of Chapter 7 (page 228)

This leaves behind the *Church Corrupt,* those who are in relationship with Jesus by profession only, or those who have an Old Covenant relationship with Him. Meaning: those who have a relationship with the written word, deferring to and obeying it, instead of having a relationship with the Spirit of Christ (the Living Word) and deferring to or obeying Him in them.

We know this is true by the parable of the talents that the one who buried the talent, had it taken away from him. He did not risk being led inspirationally by the Spirit within him, but buried the Spirit—inactive in his heart. In other words, the others who do utilize the talents given to them will go on to receive the reward of becoming celestial humans who have a role in His 1,000 year reign after being raptured. Conversely, he who buries the talent (the Holy Spirit), making inactive what little of the Spirit is embodied in him, has that talent taken from him when the Holy Spirit departs the earth. He is then made subject to the darkness of the great tribulation where there will be weeping and wailing and gnashing of teeth (Mat 25:30). The next opportunity he will have to be a part of that 1,000 year reign is to endure the great tribulation while hanging onto his testimony, not accepting the mark of the beast, or worshiping him. Then, through qualifying for the first resurrection he will once again have an opportunity to be part of the Lord's reign.

This is verified as true because of Jesus' statement to the seventh Church (age) in which He says:

NIV Rev 3:15 *I know your deeds, that you are neither cold nor hot. I wish you were either one or the other!*
NIV Rev 3:16 *So, because you are lukewarm—neither hot nor cold—I am about to spit you out of my mouth.*

What little Holy Spirit is in those He vomits out of His mouth is taken from them, and, as a result, they are left behind while the others are raptured.

Why, "vomit you out of My mouth"? Because, when you are in union with Christ, Jesus says that He is in you and you are in Him. However, Jesus says of the condition of the Church at this time, "you are neither hot nor cold." They are unfaithful and not found committed, nor do they operate in union with Jesus. On the other hand, neither have they denounced and abandoned their profession of faith in Him.

Jesus is forced to make the decision for them at this crossroad of time. At the time of the rapture, He vomits this contingency of the saints out from being "in Him." Likewise, His Spirit will be taken from them. As a result, they will be left to endure the great tribulation on their own, without any intervention from the Holy Spirit or heaven, when He withdraws from the earth without them. Meaning, no prayers will be answered during this time period, and there will be no intervention whatsoever for the saints; they are on their own.

NIV Rev 13:9 *He who has an ear, let him hear.*
NIV Rev 13:10 *If anyone is to go into captivity, into captivity he will go. If anyone is to be killed with the sword, with the sword he will be killed.*

This calls for patient endurance and faithfulness on the part of the saints.

Note: This doesn't mean that the ones He vomits out of His mouth die and go to hell, not qualified to go to heaven as many would suppose. Rather they have to endure life on earth, which will be unendurable. The earth will be a place of darkness, weeping, wailing and gnashing of teeth during the great tribulation. The saints will have the opportunity during that time on earth to prove the faithfulness of their profession by hanging onto their testimony, not worshipping the beast, or receiving his mark. If they are faithful to this, even to death, they will be counted among those who are called, "the great multitude," and are the ones who will participate in the first resurrection, becoming celestial humans. They still will reign with Christ for 1,000 years. However, they will get there the hard way and by suffer many things.

It is then that their profession of faith will finally serve them. If they stick to it, even unto death, like a butterfly coming out of a cocoon, they will be purged—metamorphized, into a celestial being at the first resurrection after a time in Hades. However, that is if they die as a result of the great tribulation. Many will survive, as horrific as it is. Those who survive and stand fast to their testimony, not worshiping the beast or taking the mark, will, at the time of the first resurrection, be raptured up into the sky with Jesus.

So, according to God's plan, the two witnesses will witness for exactly 1,260 days. Afterwards, and when they are killed, the beast will be given power for 42 months (3-1/2 years), exactly 1,260 days, to carry out his anger against the (corrupt) offspring of the woman who is clothed with the sun. At this point, the corrupt offspring is known as the whore of Babylon.

When those days come to an end, the ability of the beast to continue killing the saints will be taken away from him. The surviving saints will receive a mark on their foreheads, which will preserve their lives in the earth as well as exempt them from suffering the wrath being poured out on the world. This will look exactly like it did in Egypt. When Egypt suffered the plagues from God, the Israelites, who lived in the same place, were protected from the effects of these plagues. God will pour out His wrath upon the world as the earth changes dimensions into the spiritual realm, which is an excruciating process being used at the same time to punish the wicked. We are not told how long this process will take.

Note: Even though the surviving Christians will have a mark on their foreheads that will exempt them from the effects of God's wrath, the earth will be a terrible place to endure, either way.

Between the sixth and seventh seals combined, there is 1,260 days of the great tribulation plus an unknown amount of time in which the judgment of God is poured out upon the mortal men of the earth. This includes, first; judgment against His saints for 3-1/2 years. Then, the additional time when the judgment against the sinners of the earth who belong to the kingdom of the beast receive their punishment.

This all happens after the 3-1/2 years of hearing a final warning by the two witnesses. During that same time, the false prophet will seduce with deception as the two witnesses save. During that 3-1/2 years to come, everyone on earth will have the opportunity to decide which (S)savior they will follow. What will make the choice for them is if they decide to continue serving self and supposedly be saved from God's judgment, or decide to serve God, becoming reconciled with Him, and therefore made exempt from His judgment.

Life during the sixth and seventh seal

It is unfortunate for the saints who hold true to their testimonies and do not take the mark of the beast during the 1,260 days of the great tribulation. This is because they will need to also continue enduring life on earth during the outpouring of God's wrath, even after having gone through the great tribulation. However, they will have a mark on them from the Lord, which will not allow them to be harmed.

If they die during the great tribulation, they must remain disembodied in Hades until the days before the seventh trumpet blows and the first resurrection occurs. As for those who survive those times and receive a mark of protection from God on their foreheads, they will have to remain on the earth during the period of the wrath until they are called up to meet Jesus in the sky along with those that were resurrected; they will both be called up together.

However, when both time periods are finished and the wrath of God has been fully poured out and satisfied—in the days just before the seventh trumpet sounds and the mysteries of God will be revealed—the saints out of Hades will rise up from the dead and walk the earth again. This will further horrify the people of the earth who are of the kingdom of the beast.

In fact, every zombie movie and book made about the walking dead is inspired by the demonic view of the risen saints, anticipating this event of the dead saints rising. This includes the stories of vampires. The world will see the risen saints as blood sucking monsters from hell. As well, the beast coming alive through the image is the demonic inspiration for the story of Frankenstein.

The subjects of God's wrath will be horrified because they already have endured visitations from supernatural beings that were formerly imprisoned in Hades. For example, the locust-like creatures who will sting like scorpions and bring unbearable pain and torment for 5 months, but will not result in death. As a second example: the army of 200 million that ride horse-like creatures with heads like lions that fire, smoke, and sulfur come out of their mouths. They are to circle the globe, ravish it, and kill 1/3 of mankind.

While enduring the outpouring of wrath, with celestial monsters like these manifesting in the earth, they will be horrified when they see the great multitude of those they have killed for 1,260 days rise back to life just as the two witnesses did. In their respective stories, the walking dead survive off of eating the flesh of the living. The vampires live eternally and do not age by drinking the blood of the living. It is no coincidence that this is the case.

When the citizens of Rome considered this new religion as overtaking their empire, they would mock it and sensationalize through exaggeration the unfamiliar things they had heard that Christians practiced. The Christians had to gather to fellowship and worship God in secret and only at times that they were free to do so, for many of them were slaves. Quite often at night or early in the day (before dawn), they would gather secretly in the forests.

Christian husbands and wives considered their status of being brother and sister to each other in the family of God a higher status than that of being husband and wife. As a result, they would refer to each other, even publically, as their sister or brother (in the Lord) instead of their husband or wife.

Knowing that they will be raised from the dead, they had what the Romans would consider an irrational or obsessive concern for the dead. They treated dead bodies with the utmost respect and in all reverence, making certain that they had proper burials. This is something that the Romans really didn't understand any more than their other practices.

In addition, as a part of their worship, they practiced having communion to fulfill the Lord's command, and they would drink His blood and eat His flesh in order to live eternally. Of course it was wine that represented the blood of Christ that they drank. Likewise, it was bread that they ate to represent the flesh of Christ. For He said, in order to have eternal life, you must eat His flesh and drink His blood.

The secular world, not really understanding these Christian practices or customs, would circulate stories saying that they were a cult who met in secret during the night before the dawn. They were obsessed with the dead and they drank their blood and ate their flesh, believing that they will rise from the dead and live eternally. They were also accused of being an incestuous people who married their own brothers and sisters. These were the ignorant and slanderous ways that the Christians were beheld.

It is the truth that vampire stories and zombie stories are not just entertainment; they are preparing the world to see the resurrection of the dead who are in Christ as flesh-eating, blood-drinking, unkillable monsters from the underworld whom they should fear and run for their lives so that their flesh and blood is not consumed by them.

The truth is that after they rise from the dead (just as the two witnesses had) and sometime after they have risen, they will be called up to heaven along with those who survived these times with God's mark of protection on their foreheads. In doing so, they will transform from being mortal humans to celestial humans. Then they will return to the earth with Christ, His angels, the New Jerusalem, and all of the other saints who have received their celestial bodies. They will meet in battle against the secular people of the world, and, after defeating them, they will rule over mortal men on the earth.

However, despite what they are portrayed to be, they will not be decayed bodies from the grave who drag their limp limbs, lusting after living flesh and blood to consume. They will be beautiful, brilliant, and impervious to decay or death; they will be celestial beings of beauty and the bride of Christ.

Indeed, after this first resurrection of the dead and the call up to heaven, they will join the Lord in His return to the earth. The Lord will touch down first on the Mount of Olives, causing a great earthquake, which creates a huge valley. It will destroy the great city, Babylon, the home of the beast, which was formerly the holy city, Jerusalem. People of the kingdom of the beast will use this valley as an escape route to hide from the Messiah and the coming down of His celestial city, the New Jerusalem. All of the celestial humans and the angels will reside with the Christ inside the city on the earth.

Within the city, the light of Christ will illuminate everything. Even the celestial humans will have no need of the external light or what is known as reflective light from the sun, because all things will be illuminated for them by the light of Christ that comes out from within their celestial bodies.

However, since the earth will change dimensions from the natural universe to the spiritual realm, it will no longer have benefit of the sun by day and the stars by night. Its solar system will not come with it into the spirit realm, only the earth and its atmosphere. Also, a new sun and solar system does not await the new location in the spirit realm that the earth moves to. As such, the earth is plunged into darkness, and accordingly, so is the kingdom of the beast. Outside the city gates of the New Jerusalem, there truly will be weeping and wailing and gnashing of teeth as the people grope in the darkness of the world, reeling from all of the death and destruction that happened on the earth during the outpouring of God's wrath.

Now that His Kingdom has come to the earth, the people of the earth are threatened. The spirits of demons will enter into the mouth of the beast, the false prophet, and the Devil, who now, since the earth has been in the spirit realm, is made manifest in his form to the people of the world and can interact with them.

Hitler hid in his bunker in Berlin (not knowing when to quit) while, outside, the allied forces began to storm the city. He recruited old men, women, and children as a last ditch effort to resist the unstoppable allied forces. Likewise, the beast, the false prophet, and the Devil rally many of the survivors of the earth with their seductive speech to make a last stand fight against the heavens invading the earth (which they will behold as zombies, the walking dead who came out of their graves to feed off of their flesh and blood).

As a last ditch effort, Nimrod (the beast, who is the antichrist) finally has his battle against God which he has longed for and boasted about even 4,000 years ago. The beast, false prophet, and Devil falsely inspire the people by telling them that if they all unite together, they can once again defeat the Lord and eject Him out of the earth. Just as they did previously when they killed the two witnesses and the Holy Spirit withdrew along with His people. In doing so, they are thereby protecting themselves from any further judgments of God so that they may live lives of their own choosing, serving themselves. After they gather this great army around the globe with Nimrod in the front, they step onto the ground of battle, which is the place known as Armageddon.

This is the biggest and most pitiful shame in the entire history of mankind, as well as the greatest deception. For with the sounding of the seventh trumpet comes the end of God's wrath punishing the inhabitants of the earth for their sins. The horror of judgment has finished. Jesus, the Christ, is here on the earth to establish His Kingdom of peace across the globe and to take over the governments of the world. He will heal the earth, restore the people of it, and bring the bliss of His Kingdom for 1,000 years.

However, the beast, the false prophet, the Devil, and the kings of the earth don't want to give up their power. So they seduce the people into believing that it is not over and that they must desperately gather together to defeat these invaders from the spirit realm.

The Lord gives warnings in the Bible about this moment, admonishing the people to hang on, be patient, guard their lives just a little while longer because they have come to the end of hell on earth. If they were able to survive the horrors of the sixth and seventh seal, then they should hang on just a little longer, because they will be able to go from the most horrifying times the earth has ever endured to the most blissful time the earth will ever experience as a result of the reign of Christ. They will be blessed if they are patient, lay low, and survive while waiting for the end of the outpouring of wrath.

This is opposed to losing it because they are so overwhelmed with the outpouring of God's wrath they no longer see God as a good God, forgetting they are only receiving what they deserve, but end up hating Him and seeing Him as the source of everything bad. As a result, they end up not waiting out the last few days but, in their hatred, join the beast in fighting God at the battle of Armageddon, and then die.

If they, instead, hang on to their cool and wait it out, they will reach the end of the wrath and make it to the most blissful time on earth since the garden, instead of dying only days before it comes.

NIV Rev 16:14 They are spirits of demons performing miraculous signs, and they go out to the kings of the whole world, to gather them for the battle on the great day of God Almighty.
NIV Rev 16:15 "Behold, I come like a thief! Blessed is he who stays awake and keeps his clothes with him, so that he may not go naked and be shamefully exposed."
NIV Rev 16:16 Then they gathered the kings together to the place that in Hebrew is called Armageddon.

Again, in verse 14, Jesus is talking about the very end of the outpouring of His wrath. He warns that the beast will seduce many into fighting Him at Armageddon.

Verse 15 says, "he who stays awake and keeps his clothes with him, so that he may not go naked and be shamefully exposed." This would be better translated as: he who stays awake and guards his clothes so he won't be caught shamefully naked, as some translations do say.

This would be a weird place for Jesus to warn us thinking that presumably we would be running around naked, and, if so, we should keep our clothes close by because we don't know when He might appear. He doesn't say, stay dressed so that you don't show the shame of your nakedness. He says, keep your clothes close by so that you don't show the shame of your nakedness. As if, with all that is going on, this is the most important thing we should be worried about—to keep our clothes close by so we can hurry up and get dressed if we see Jesus coming on a cloud. Otherwise the whole world will see us naked, because we might not get dressed quick enough if our clothes are too far away.

I guess that would be like your mother telling you to put on clean underwear in the morning in case you get hit by a car and die later that day and someone will find out you have skid marks on your underwear, which (by inference), is far worse a problem than death.

Clothes for the soul is a person's body. A soul is clothed in a body, or the body embodies the soul. In the previous verse 14, Jesus just warned us that we can be seduced by the beast into fighting the returning Jesus. Yet, this would result in death, because everyone who comes to fight Jesus will be killed by the breath of His mouth. He is, in essence, saying the same thing that He spoke in Daniel: guard your life, don't be seduced into fighting Him. If you are, you will become naked—unclothed—disembodied, in other words, dead! And shamefully so, because as soon as that battle is over, all of the problems in the earth will be over and bliss will prevail, and you will not be a part of this. Instead, you will be shamefully disembodied (naked) in Hades. Then verse 16 finishes His warning by saying, then they gathered for battle at Armageddon. Jesus doesn't want to kill any more mortal men than He has to, so He lets us know how crucial that moment will be and how important our decision is if we make it that far.

Whatever they choose, those who choose to fight the ultimate battle will gather at Armageddon. Then, Jesus will come out of the city and greet them in battle. Out of the breath of His mouth, which has been also referred to as a sword, and in a single act, all who are gathered there against Him will perish; they will die! It is now time for, "the great supper of God" to begin for every scavenger bird there is. They will feast off of the bodies of the dead who were not patient and did not wait to see that their troubles were, in fact, over, but instead, opposed the coming Christ.

Every single one of those who came to fight will die, with the exception of the beast (known as the antichrist), the false prophet, and the Devil. Their fate is this: the Devil is imprisoned in the Abyss for 1,000 years and then loosed in the earth for a short time. The beast and the false prophet, who have already served their time in Hades, and were resurrected from the dead, will finally meet their decreed fate of suffering a second death. They will be thrown alive into the lake of fire for all of eternity. They will be alone—its first two citizens. No one will join them for at least 1,000 years and after the last day of judgment.

At this time (the last day of judgment), those who are deemed suitable and are declared sheep because of their deeds will go on to live eternally with the rest of the celestial humans who reigned with Christ. The day of judgment will be preceded by the entire natural universe (the earth and every mortal thing within it) being thrown into the lake of fire with the sound of a loud crash. The mortals on the earth at the time will become suddenly disembodied and will be resurrected with a new body so that they may face the throne of judgment and be sorted out as sheep or goats.

After the goats are thrown alive into the lake of fire to experience their second death, a new heavens and a new earth will appear, and upon it will be the New Jerusalem. This city will be decked out to dress the bride, housing the countless celestial humans who are the bride of Christ. The sheep who are given celestial bodies on the last day will live on the new earth with their Prince, King Jesus, and His bride, who together will occupy the New Jerusalem. The sheep will be His citizens and part of the greater family of God. Together they all will live for eternity in the bliss of His Kingdom. Amen, and amen!

Again, we must digress to finish up the verses of the seven seals.

We rejoin the seventh seal after the half an hour of silence (inactivity) comes to an end.

NIV Rev 8:2 And I saw the seven angels who stand before God, and to them were given seven trumpets.

Note: In the book of Revelation, the story of the judgment of fire is told four different times, just as the Gospel is. The first account starts with verse 6:1—the seven seals ending at 11:19. The second account starts with verse 12:1—the woman clothed with the sun (*the Church Pure*) and the dragon—which ends at 16:21. The third account starts with verse 17:1—the woman (*the Church Corrupt*) and the beast—and ends with 21:8. The fourth account starts with verse 21:9—the New Jerusalem—and goes to the end of the book. This last account is the shortest account, because it starts with the New Jerusalem which really is the end of the story but is also what the whole story is leading to and the destiny of those redeemed during the process of the judgment of fire.

Each of the four times that the story of Revelation is told, there is a different emphasis, which necessitates a different starting point. As the different accounts are told, the starting points of the next start progressively deeper into the story. However, all four accounts bring us all the way to the very end. Each time it is told, however, each next account gives increasingly more information about the end of the story.

Each time the story is told, it obviously reviews most of the things told in the other accounts, like the Gospels. However, direct reference is not usually made in a way that makes it easy to relate what one story is saying about the same matter to what the other stories are describing. Most often, completely different wording and information is used in one account to describe the same person or event as in the others. As such, it makes it challenging to match up the four different accounts.

However, there is a huge advantage to this! Every time we read of a different account of the same person or event, we can gather more information about that person or event, thereby making our understanding deeper and giving us a clearer picture of Revelation. The trick, however, is being able to match up the accounts so that you know when their different information is talking about the same person or event as the others.

Let's give an example. The second beast out of the earth in verses 13:11-18 is described as having two horns like a lamb but speaks like a dragon. He is described as paving the way for the beast out of the water and doing astonishing things, exercising power on behalf of the first beast. In this account and with these verses dedicated to introducing us to this person, we know him only as the second beast who came out of the earth (the grave).

Then, in the other accounts in Revelation, he is not referred to as the second beast who came out of the earth. There are three other occasions where he is referred to in the book of Revelation. Those three subsequent times, he is referred to as the "false prophet" and there is no mention of him being the second beast.

In fact, this person is mentioned in the book of Daniel also. There he is referred to as, "the other prince who will come." (Amp Da 9:26). We are told there that he makes treaties with the nations, which kicks off the beginning of last seven. Then, at the midpoint of the last seven (3-1/2 years in), he stops the sacrifices in the temple. After another 1,290 days, the last seven has concluded, and he sets up an image of the antichrist in the Holy temple. He then commits abominations which cause the beast to appear from among the dead, and, in turn, who will make the earth desolate for 3-1/2 years (42 months) until the power of the holy people (the Church) is broken.

In the book of Revelation, he is mentioned four times. Three of those times he is called by a different name from the first, but what is said about him is consistent with his description in the account which introduces us to him calling him the second beast. When we recognize the false prophet as one and the same as the "second beast who comes up out of the earth", and as the "other prince who will come," the different names and their subsequent information gives us a better picture of exactly who this person is and what role he has in the end times.

The reason the above note is important is to point out that, in the first account, when the story of the judgment of fire is told through the seven seals, the story ends with the seven trumpet blasts which release the wrath of God on the world. However, in the second account, this same event of the seven trumpet blasts are referred to as the seven bowls of God's wrath. They are speaking of the same event—the outpouring of God's wrath on the earth.

Here are a couple of things that are important about this outpouring of God's wrath. First, there is a reason the seventh and final seal releases seven trumpets. And when the event is repeated in the second account, it is referred to as seven bowls. This is because of the importance and meaning of the number seven. Seven means completion and divine perfection.

When we hear the first account of the judgment of fire through the seven seals, we are hearing the sevenness, or complete story, from beginning to end and the perfection of His plan. None of the other three accounts frame the story within the *structure of sevens*. This is because the other accounts do not tell the complete story, but start at different points in the story as a whole. They start where the emphasis or subject of that account finally becomes a part of the story.

When the wrath of God is poured out on the world who hated God and His people, He wants us to know that His wrath is perfect and complete, lacking nothing, leaving nothing undone or unaccounted for. This is why, in both cases, they are broken down and described according to the sevenness of His wrath (seven trumpets, and seven bowls) or within the *structure of sevens*. All accounts are settled and perfect justice has been served.

Secondly, this is not a purifying, redeeming act like the first 3-1/2 years (which was the great tribulation). No, this is simply an outpouring of punishment and judgment that brings condemnation to those who suffer it and a total end to everything that is evil.

You could say that God's wrath is a purifying act of the earth in the sense that God's wrath is preparing the earth to have an ability to interact with the celestial dimension so that Jesus, His celestial humans, and angels can rule it. Likewise, it is being purified in the sense of being purged of every trace of the human authority that rules it with its Babylonian system of enslavement of the people. It is even being purged of the authority and people who hate God and His people, making way for the government of the Christ. However, it is not a redeeming work for the people it is poured out on. Their death as a result of God's wrath will not serve to make them part of the great multitude in heaven, but, instead, reserve them in a hellish place in Hades to be resurrected, judged, and suffer a second death by being thrown alive into the lake of fire.

NIV Rev 8:3 *Another angel, who had a golden censer, came and stood at the altar. He was given much incense to offer, with the prayers of all the saints, on the golden altar before the throne.*

The prayers that are referred to are the prayers of those at the fifth seal who were killed because of their love for God and were asking how long before God will avenge their death, including that of Christ. These prayers accumulate, adding to their numbers those who die after the cross and until the end of the great tribulation.

NIV Rev 8:4 *The smoke of the incense, together with the prayers of the saints, went up before God from the angel's hand.*
NIV Rev 8:5 *Then the angel took the censer, filled it with fire from the altar, and hurled it on the earth; and there came peals of thunder, rumblings, flashes of lightning and an earthquake.*

Verse 5 gives us a description of what the answered prayers look like from heaven looking down, however, what is described as happening during the seven trumpet blasts is what it looks like from the earth looking up, being the recipient of the censor hurled at it.

The Day of the Lord Is Coming

NLT 2Pe 3:1 *This is my second letter to you, dear friends, and in both of them I have tried to stimulate your wholesome thinking and refresh your memory.*
NLT 2Pe 3:2 *I want you to remember and understand what the holy prophets said long ago and what our Lord and Savior commanded through your apostles.*
NLT 2Pe 3:3 *First, I want to remind you that in the last days there will be scoffers who will laugh at the truth and do every evil thing they desire.*

NLT 2Pe 3:4 This will be their argument: "Jesus promised to come back, did he? Then where is he? Why, as far back as anyone can remember, everything has remained exactly the same since the world was first created."

NLT 2Pe 3:5 They deliberately forget that God made the heavens by the word of his command, and he brought the earth up from the water and surrounded it with water.

NLT 2Pe 3:6 Then he used the water to destroy the world with a mighty flood.

NLT 2Pe 3:7 And God has also commanded that the heavens and the earth will be consumed by fire on the day of judgment, when ungodly people will perish.

NLT 2Pe 3:8 But you must not forget, dear friends, that a day is like a thousand years to the Lord, and a thousand years is like a day.

NLT 2Pe 3:9 The Lord isn't really being slow about his promise to return, as some people think. No, he is being patient for your sake. He does not want anyone to perish, so he is giving more time for everyone to repent.

NLT 2Pe 3:10 But the day of the Lord will come as unexpectedly as a thief. Then the heavens will pass away with a terrible noise, and everything in them will disappear in fire, and the earth and everything on it will be exposed to judgment.

NLT 2Pe 3:11 Since everything around us is going to melt away, what holy, godly lives you should be living!

NLT 2Pe 3:12 You should look forward to that day and hurry it along—the day when God will set the heavens on fire and the elements will melt away in the flames.

NLT 2Pe 3:13 But we are looking forward to the new heavens and new earth he has promised, a world where everyone is right with God.

NLT 2Pe 3:14 And so, dear friends, while you are waiting for these things to happen, make every effort to live a pure and blameless life. And be at peace with God.

NLT 2Pe 3:15 And remember, the Lord is waiting so that people have time to be saved. This is just as our beloved brother Paul wrote to you with the wisdom God gave him—

NLT 2Pe 3:16 speaking of these things in all of his letters. Some of his comments are hard to understand, and those who are ignorant and unstable have twisted his letters around to mean something quite different from what he meant, just as they do the other parts of Scripture—and the result is disaster for them.

NLT 2Pe 3:17 *I am warning you ahead of time, dear friends, so that you can watch out and not be carried away by the errors of these wicked people. I don't want you to lose your own secure footing.*

NLT 2Pe 3:18 *But grow in the special favor and knowledge of our Lord and Savior Jesus Christ. To him be all glory and honor, both now and forevermore. Amen.*

And amen!

Timeline

The Last Seven to the Reign of Christ

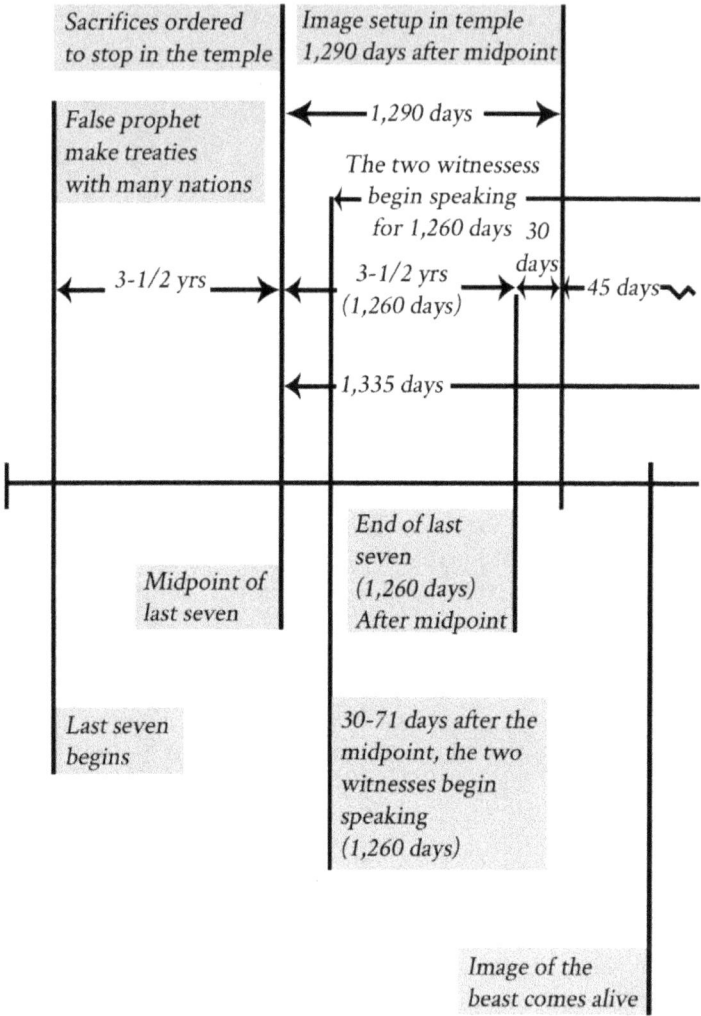

Sacrifices ordered to stop in the temple

Image setup in temple 1,290 days after midpoint

False prophet make treaties with many nations

1,290 days

The two witnessess begin speaking for 1,260 days 30 days

3-1/2 yrs

3-1/2 yrs (1,260 days)

45 days

1,335 days

Midpoint of last seven

End of last seven (1,260 days) After midpoint

Last seven begins

30-71 days after the midpoint, the two witnesses begin speaking (1,260 days)

Image of the beast comes alive

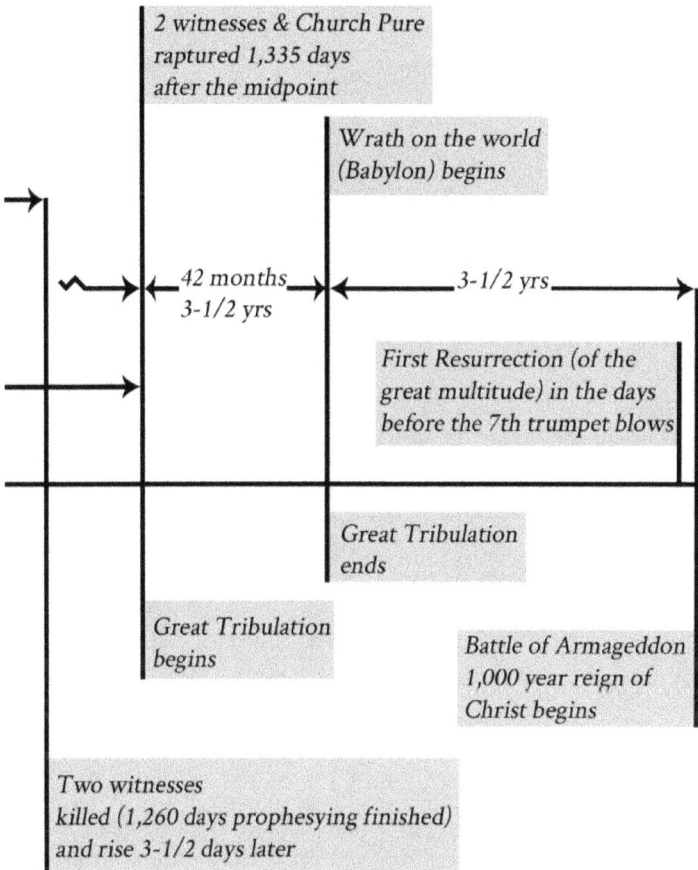

2 witnesses & Church Pure
raptured 1,335 days
after the midpoint

Wrath on the world
(Babylon) begins

←42 months→ ←————3-1/2 yrs————→
3-1/2 yrs

First Resurrection (of the
great multitude) in the days
before the 7th trumpet blows

Great Tribulation
ends

Great Tribulation
begins

Battle of Armageddon
1,000 year reign of
Christ begins

Two witnesses
killed (1,260 days prophesying finished)
and rise 3-1/2 days later

Bibliography

Amplified Bible. Scripture quotations marked (Amp) are taken from the Amplified Bible, Copyright © 1954, 1958, 1962, 1964, 1965, 1987 by The Lockman Foundation. Used by permission.

Chinese. (2014). Retrieved September 2015, from Bible Probe: www.bibleprobe.com/chinese.htm

Flavius Josephus of the Antiquities of the Jews-Book 1. (n.d.). Retrieved September 2015, from penelope.uchicago.edu: penelope.uchicago.edu/josephus/ant-1.html

(n.d.). Kitāb Al-Magāll or The Book of the Rolls. In *One of the Books of Clement.* Retrieved from http://www.sacred-texts.com/chr/aa/aa2.htm

Livingston, P., & Livingston, C. (2015). *Christianity: A Lost Civilization* Wauconda: The Naked Apostles.

New American Standard. Scripture quotations marked (NAS) are taken from the NEW AMERICAN STANDARD BIBLE®, Copyright © 1960,1962,1963,1968,1971,1972,1973,1975,1977,1995 by The Lockman Foundation. Used by permission.

New International Version. Scriptures taken from the Holy Bible, New International Version®, NIV®. Copyright © 1973, 1978, 1984 by Biblica, Inc.™ Used by permission of Zondervan. All rights reserved worldwide. www.zondervan.com The "NIV" and "New International Version" are trademarks registered in the United States Patent and Trademark Office by Biblica, Inc.™

New Living Translation. Holy Bible, New Living Translation copyright © 1996, 2004, 2007 by Tyndale House Foundation. Used by permission of Tyndale House Publishers Inc., Carol Stream, Illinois 60188. All rights reserved. New Living, NLT, and the New Living Translation logo are registered` trademarks of Tyndale House Publishers.

Nimrod. (n.d.). Retrieved September 2015, from Jewish Encyclopedia: http://www.jewishencyclopedia.com/articles/11548-nimrod

Nimrod. (n.d.). Retrieved September 2015, from Wikipedia: The Free Encyclopedia: https://en.wikipedia.org/wiki/Nimrod

Rogers, D. M. (2011, April). *The Truth about Easter.* Retrieved September 2015, from BibleTruth.cc: http://www.bibletruth.cc/Easter.htm#The_Ancient_Practice_of_th e_40_Day_Fasting_and_Weeping

World English Bible. Scripture quotations marked (WEB) are taken from The World English Bible, which is in the public domain. Special thanks to Michael Paul Johnson and all who worked on the translation as a means to release a modern version of the Bible that is available for non-copyright use. A reminder that the Bible is not owned by man.

ABOUT THE AUTHORS

We are just a voice

WEB Jn 1:19 *This is John's testimony (about himself), when the Jews sent priests and Levites from Jerusalem to ask him, "Who are you?"*
WEB Jn 1:20 *He declared, and didn't deny, but he declared, "I am not the Christ."*
WEB Jn 1:21 *They asked him, "What then? Are you Elijah?"*
He said, "I am not."
"Are you the prophet?"
He answered, "No."
WEB Jn 1:22 *They said therefore to him, "Who are you? Give us an answer to take back to those who sent us. What do you say about yourself?"*
WEB Jn 1:23 *He said, "**I am the voice** of one crying in the wilderness, 'Make straight the way of the Lord . . ."*

True prophets in the Bible did not convince people who they were; in fact, they refused to talk about themselves. They refused to bring credibility to the words of God they spoke by trying to get people to believe who they were and trust them. They knew that it would be profaning the words of God to do so, and it would be elevating themselves above God's words. They knew that God's words have their own credibility because they are from God. And God will show them (His own words) as from Him.

God's prophets also knew that those who truly love God will, therefore, benefit from their words, and those who are lovers of themselves will not benefit from them, because they will be dismissive and not trust them. The time is over that we look at the person who speaks to decide if we believe. We must begin to discern if the words are from God and if they carry God's Spirit.

You might say to that, "but not everyone can discern God." If that is the case, then they indict themselves as not being "known" by Jesus. They unwittingly reveal about themselves that they desire to do their own will and not the Lord's, just as the religious leaders who wanted Jesus to prove His credibility so they could decide if His words were from God.

Amp Jn 7:16 Jesus answered them by saying, My teaching is not My own, but His Who sent Me.

Amp Jn 7:17 If any man desires to do His will (God's pleasure), he will know (have the needed illumination to recognize, and can tell for himself) whether the teaching is from God or whether I am speaking from Myself and of My own accord and on My own authority.

Many will think this is an oversimplified notion. However, it is so simple that it is not only true but reveals a simple but foundational truth about the person. What Jesus is saying is that if a man has a pure heart and wants to do the will of God above his own will, then what seems intuitively right (what sets well with that man) will be God's will and His words. However, even if you are a scholar, theologian, or work in the field of religion, and you desire to carry out your own will, having your own agendas and ambitions, well then, what seems right to that man is not God's will or His words, but that which lines up with his own will.

Generally speaking, the greatest religious minds in the world judge if something is from God by looking at the standing and qualifications of the man speaking them. In the above case, Jesus shows they may be smart in their own eyes, believing they know what is from God and therefore able to judge according to their knowledge of God. However, that would be saying in effect, we know everything about God because of our great knowledge. Therefore, if you say anything outside of our knowledge of God, or outside of the knowledge base of the accepted theological models, or if you are not a qualified student of those accepted models, then we must deduce your words are not from God.

To Jesus, they show about themselves that they don't recognize His words as from God because of their personal acquaintance with God. Instead, they have to judge by facts. They show themselves as having no real relationship with God; they would not recognize Him when He stands right before them. As a matter of fact, on another occasion when they showed contempt for Him, Jesus said of them:

NIV Jn 5:42 . . . *but I know you. I know that you do not have the love of God in your hearts.*

They were once again wanting Him to prove who He was, and what right He had to talk the way He did. Jesus, instead of being intimidated, marveled at how He spoke and acted out everything the Father willed, yet they did not recognize His words as His Father's. Furthermore, they were, by nature, hostile and offended towards those words.

Let's look at that closer through an illustration. For example, you have a woman who claims to be married to a man named Jim. Then, a man claiming to be Jim and her husband approaches her. The above case is like the wife doubting this man is her husband. So then, she begins to question him. For example, "If you're Jim, when were you born?" And, "What kind of car did you have when you first got your license?" If he doesn't answer to her satisfaction, she decides that he is not her husband Jim. This might seem reasonable, and if he got the answers incorrect or didn't remember, the people listening might believe her when she says, "this is not my husband."

If there was anybody in the crowd that had wisdom, they might say this begs another question, "Hey lady, are you really Jim's wife or are you an imposter?" The reasoning of the wise man is, do you really need factual evidence to know if he is your husband? Don't you know your husband when he is standing right in front of you? Jesus is marveling at the religious leaders who are supposed to know God and claim to be in union with Him. However, they don't recognize Him when He stands before them. They don't even recognize His words as from God. Do they really need factual evidence to know something that they are supposed to have intimate knowledge of? Next question, why does it not occur to anyone to question if these men of God, leaders of the Jewish faith, may be imposters because they don't judge if someone and their words are from God by their intimate knowledge of God? They need factual evidence?

What did that tell Jesus? It told Him that even the top religious leaders who know the written word by heart can't recognize God when they stand right in front of Him. It told Him that they were, in their inner man, hostile and threatened by God's words. It told Him that, in their inner selves, they really had no love or even any natural attraction towards God, His heart, and the Spirit of His words. They were obviously naturally repelled by them; they had no real love for God and their response showed it. However, to the religious leaders, they thought themselves wise and discerning to hold Jesus and His words suspect by judging Him with factual evidence. How disappointing it must have been to Jesus that the best of the best had no intimate knowledge of God and they were repulsed by Him when facing Him. Yes, Jesus' deduction was correct, there was no love of God in their hearts.

It is a Biblical fact that the major way we will be judged is it will be proven if we have a natural attraction to please God and do His will, therefore saying about us that we love Him more than ourselves. Learning by the folly of the leaders and the scholarly of Jesus' day, it is not by a knowledgeable and scholarly mind that one can successfully judge or discern what words coming from what person are from God or not. You can't judge superficially. No, it takes something much greater than to know every Bible verse by heart and to be able to have insightful knowledge of the person speaking them. It actually takes something much harder to attain than perfect scholarly knowledge of the written word. It takes a pure heart. Not meaning a sinless heart, but one which is single-minded, wanting to please God by serving Him and wanting to do His will at the expense of their own. This is what qualifies one to recognize if something is from God.

WEB Mt 5:8 *Blessed are the pure in heart, for they shall see God.*

It is true that as Colleen and I gain a larger following of our teachings and ministry, people will undoubtedly come to know us personally, and what kind of people we are. However, as teachers, we teach people how to live as spiritual men and women, discerning life in a spiritual way.

We have found the best way to teach discerning of spirit. It is not by knowing how to figure people out or to train them to have a spiritual power. No, we teach them to be single-minded when it comes to God, to be surrendered to His will in a pure or holistic way.

Having a still spirit which is not agitated with passions will create a huge contrast. The contrast of having the stillness of God's Spirit rule your heart coming in contact with the agitated spirit energies the people of this world operate out of makes one sensitive to discern spirit.

Jesus was right; wanting to do God's will with all your heart alone will cause you to recognize if one has God's Spirit in them and if they speak word's which are from God. As the saying goes, "You can't cheat an honest man."

NIV Jn 8:15 *You judge by human standards...*

NIV Jn 7:24 *Stop judging by mere appearances, and make a right judgment."*

As such, Colleen and I would like to be known first as a voice, just a voice. We want the words we speak from God to have more prominence and have their own credibility, than that of who we are. Therefore, we don't want to propagate people judging superficially if one is from God by giving our Bio. We want the words we speak to be more important than who we are. We want those who have a pure heart in wanting to serve God to check in their heart if we and the words we speak are from God.

We want those who don't have a pure heart to have a change of heart so they may know for themselves the voice and words of God when they hear them. However, we want to point people in the way to properly discern so they may know for themselves if we are from God and speak His words; in the same way John the Baptist tried to convey. You ask about us, and we will tell you about Him. You insist on wanting to know about us, and we will then tell you, we are just a voice making way for the One you should know and should be asking about. We are not a face or a name or people you should want to know, we are just a voice which gives voice to the One whose words you need to know.

OTHER BOOKS BY THE NAKED APOSTLES

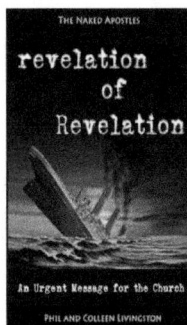

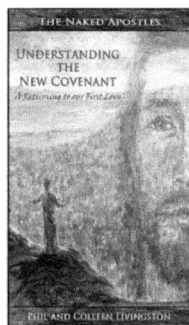

www.ingramcontent.com/pod-product-compliance
Lightning Source LLC
LaVergne TN
LVHW051044080426
835508LV00019B/1697